United States
Department of
Agriculture

Forest Service

Southern
Research Station

General Technical
Report SRS–149

Urban Forests of Tennessee, 2009

David J. Nowak, Anne B. Cumming,
Daniel Twardus, Robert E. Hoehn, III,
Christopher M. Oswalt, and Thomas J. Brandeis

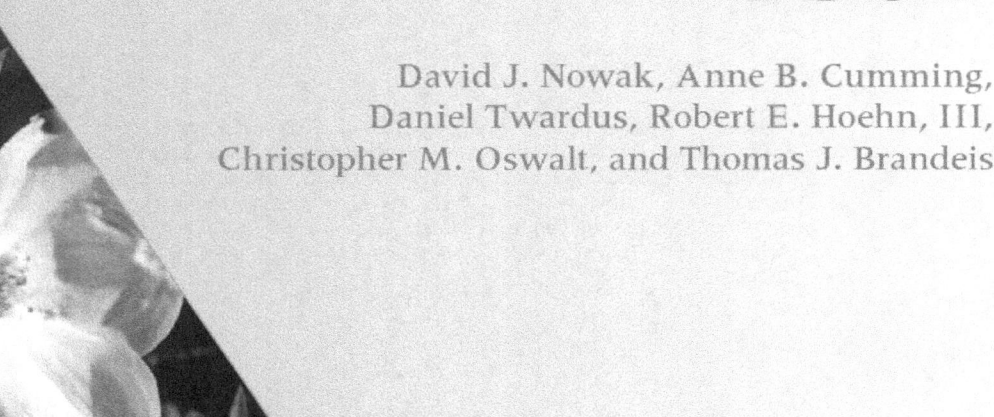

Authors

David J. Nowak, Research Forester and Project Leader, U.S. Department of Agriculture Forest Service, Northern Research Station, Syracuse, NY 13210;

Anne B. Cumming, Forester, **Daniel Twardus,** Forest Health Group Leader, U.S. Department of Agriculture Forest Service, State and Private Forestry, Morgantown, WV 26505;

Robert E. Hoehn, III, Forester, U.S. Department of Agriculture Forest Service, Northern Research Station, Syracuse, NY 13210;

Christopher M. Oswalt, Research Forester, **Thomas J. Brandeis,** Research Forester, U.S. Department of Agriculture Forest Service, Southern Research Station, Knoxville, TN 37919.

Urban parks are wonderful urban forest landscapes that provide aesthetic beauty and often provide a venue for art displays for additional enjoyment. (photo by Christopher M. Oswalt)

Front cover: top (hex): The annual Dogwood Arts Festival in Knoxville, TN celebrates one of the common tree species in Tennessee urban forests, the flowering dogwood. (photo by Christopher M. Oswalt); middle (circle): The campus of Vanderbilt University contains a beautiful urban forest landscape offering multiple benefits to attending students and the citizens of Nashville, TN. (photo courtesy Google Images); bottom (triangle): A flowering dogwood in full bloom in a west central Tennessee urban forest. (photo by Christopher M. Oswalt)

January 2012
Southern Research Station
200 W.T. Weaver Blvd.
Asheville, NC 28804

Urban Forests of Tennessee, 2009

David J. Nowak, Anne B. Cumming,
Daniel Twardus, Robert E. Hoehn, III,
Christopher M. Oswalt, and Thomas J. Brandeis

Steven G. Scott

This study is the first statewide inventory and forest health monitoring effort to quantify the urban forests within the State of Tennessee. It represents a snapshot in time of the extent and condition of trees and forests in urban areas where a majority of people live in Tennessee. Towns, cities, and communities are sheltered by trees and forests providing them many environmental and economic benefits and uses.

Perhaps the most significant feature of an urban forest is its immediate impact on the use of energy and savings we incur as a result of the shadowing effect of trees near homes, businesses, and industrial areas. These savings already amount to over $66 million per year in Tennessee and could be much greater with continued care and maintenance of our urban forests. Other real benefits of urban trees and forest include air and water purification services, with air filtering provided by trees valued at over $204 million per year. So many of these functional values of the urban forest go unrecognized and unreported. This report, for the first time, puts a face on this urban resource and what it means to the State in terms of economic and environmental values.

We could lose this resource very easily without proper care and maintenance. Trees succumb to age, insect, disease, and the harsh growing environment of urban spaces. Much can be done to preserve this resource and ensure that the functional benefits of urban trees and forests continue for many generations in Tennessee. It starts with careful measurement and inventory of this key natural resource. This report is the first attempt to do so.

This report was accomplished through generous funding provided by the USDA Forest Service and the State. Many days and hours were spent collecting tree data in backyards, industrial sites, playgrounds, and small groves of trees. Please examine this report carefully and see for yourself what a great resource our urban forests are, and find in these pages your opportunity to ensure their continued health and productivity. Urban forests truly are working forests.

Sincerely,

Steven G. Scott
Tennessee State Forester
Tennessee Division of Forestry

Contents

Abstract

Trees in cities can contribute significantly to human health and environmental quality. Unfortunately, little is known about the urban forest resource in the State of Tennessee and what it contributes locally and regionally in terms of ecology, economy, and social well-being. In an effort to better understand this resource and its values, the U.S. Department of Agriculture (USDA) Forest Service, Forest Inventory and Analysis, Forest Health, and Urban and community Forestry programs, in partnership with USDA Forest Service research and the Tennessee Department of Agriculture, Division of Forestry, initiated a pilot study to sample trees within all urban areas across the State. Urban forest structure, functions, health, and values in Tennessee were analyzed using the i-Tree Eco (formerly Urban Forest Effects) model. Results reveal urban areas in Tennessee have an estimated 284 million trees in urban areas with canopies that cover 37.7 percent of the area. Most trees are found in forested areas (56 percent) with the most common species being Chinese privet, Virginia pine, and eastern redcedar. Yellow-poplar, chestnut oak, and white oak were the top three species in terms of basal area, while hackberry, yellow-poplar, and flowering dogwood were the top three in terms of leaf area. Tennessee's urban forests currently store about 16.9 million tons of carbon valued at $350 million. In addition, these trees remove about 890,000 tons of carbon per year ($18.4 million per year) and about 27,100 tons of pollution per year ($203.9 million per year). Trees in urban Tennessee are estimated to reduce annual residential energy costs by $66 million per year. The structural, or compensatory, value is estimated at $79 billion. Overall, 9.4 percent of the sampled trees were within maintained areas. Land uses with the highest proportion of trees in maintained areas were agriculture, residential, and commercial/industrial. Overall, 1.8 percent of trees found were standing dead. Species with at least 100,000 trees in the population with the highest percent of its population in dead trees were sassafras (17.3 percent), black locust (14.7 percent), and black walnut (14.0 percent). Species with highest percent crown dieback were black walnut, sassafras, and shagbark hickory. Information in this report can be used to advance the understanding and management of urban forests to improve human health and environmental quality in Tennessee.

Keywords: Air pollution removal, carbon sequestration, ecosystem services, FIA, tree value, urban forestry.

Urban Forests of Tennessee, 2009

David J. Nowak, Anne B. Cumming, Daniel Twardus, Robert E. Hoehn, III, Christopher M. Oswalt, and Thomas J. Brandeis

Highlights

Value

- Urban vegetation, particularly trees, provides numerous benefits that can improve environmental quality and human health in and around urban areas.

- Tennessee's urban forests are working for the citizens of the State and are currently valued at about $80 billion.

- Urban forests in Tennessee currently provide functional values of >$350 million in carbon storage, $18.4 million per year in additional annual carbon sequestration, $203.9 million per year in pollution removal, and $66 million per year in building energy use reductions.

Area

- There were a total of 1.6 million acres of urban land in Tennessee.

- The land use that covered the largest area within the urban boundary was transportation followed by residential.

- About 234,000 acres within the urban boundary are considered forest land by the Forest Inventory and Analysis program.

Trees

- In Tennessee's urban areas there are an estimated 284.1 million trees.

- An estimated 160.2 million trees were found in forest areas, 44.2 million within transportation corridors, 37.6 million on residential lands, 21.8 million on "other" urban land uses, 14.2 million on agricultural lands, and 6.2 million on commercial/industrial lands.

- The most common tree species observed in Tennessee urban areas were Chinese privet, Virginia pine, and eastern redcedar. By comparison, the most common tree species found statewide are red maple, yellow-poplar (the State tree), and sweetgum.

- For trees ≤5 inches diameter at breast height (d.b.h.), the common species were Chinese privet, Virginia pine, and flowering dogwood.

- For trees >5 inches d.b.h., the common species were eastern redcedar, hackberry, and Virginia pine.

- A total of 99 tree species were encountered within urban forests whereas 117 species were encountered on all forest land across the State.

- A little over 9 percent of trees were classified as growing in maintained areas.

- Of the "maintained" trees, the most common species were flowering dogwood, hackberry, and Chinese privet.

Urban Forest Health

- Overall, about 1.8 percent of the total urban tree population was standing dead.

- Black walnut was the tree species with the highest average percent crown dieback.

- The most common damages on trees were trunk bark inclusions and vines growing in tree crowns. However, no single damage class impacted >9 percent of the total urban tree population.

- Potential risks from exotic pests included the recently discovered thousand cankers disease, which impacts black walnut; hemlock woolly adelgid, which defoliates hemlocks; the Asian longhorned beetle that kills a wide range of hardwood species; and the emerald ash borer that has recently been discovered in east Tennessee.

Executive Summary

Data from 255 field plots located within the urban areas (U.S. Department of Commerce 2000 definition) of Tennessee were analyzed in this pilot project. Trees within the urban boundary were sampled according to the U.S. Department of Agriculture (USDA) Forest Service, Forest Inventory and Analysis (FIA) and Forest Health Monitoring programs' protocols with modifications between 2005 and 2009. Data were analyzed using the Forest Service's i-Tree Eco (formerly Urban Forest Effects) model to quantify and describe the benefits of the Tennessee urban forest. The data from this project will help fill a national data gap related to trees within urban areas and help provide data on ecosystem services and values provided by urban forests.

The FIA grid of one plot every 6,000 acres was used to determine plot locations within the urban boundary. These plot locations were obtained with permission from the USDA Forest Service, Southern Research Station, FIA program. Some of these plots within the urban area are part of a national system to inventory and monitor forest and timber lands. The remaining plots were newly established plots to allow for a comprehensive assessment of the urban forest area (See Methods for a full description).

In Tennessee's urban areas there are an estimated 284.1 million trees with 160.2 million in forest areas (56.4 percent of trees), 44.2 million within transportation corridors (15.5 percent), 37.6 million on residential lands (13.2 percent), 21.8 million on "other" urban land uses (7.7 percent), 14.2 million on agricultural lands (5.0 percent), and 6.2 million on commercial/industrial lands (2.2 percent) (table 1). The most common species were: Chinese privet (10.4 percent of the population), Virginia pine (6.0 percent), eastern redcedar (6.0 percent), hackberry (5.2 percent), and flowering dogwood (4.9 percent). Species that dominated in terms of leaf area were: hackberry (6.9 percent), yellow-poplar (the State tree) (5.4 percent), eastern redcedar (4.5 percent), flowering dogwood (4.5 percent), and red maple (4.3 percent).

Forest health data collected on crown conditions and occurrence of damage indicates that the urban forests of Tennessee are healthy and vigorous. However, risks to the urban forest exist. The thousand cankers disease is a recently discovered insect-disease complex that kills black walnuts and could affect the 1.2 million black walnuts found in Tennessee's urban forests in addition to threatening an additional 28 million black walnut trees in Tennessee growing outside of the urban boundary. The hemlock woolly adelgid could also impact the estimated 66,000 hemlock trees in urban Tennessee. Additionally, the emerald ash borer poses a risk to 1.8 percent of the trees in Tennessee's urban forests, while the Asian longhorned beetle could infest > 25 percent of the trees in urban areas.

The 284.1 million urban trees in Tennessee have an estimated structural value of $79 billion, provide an annual energy saving to residents of $66 million, remove $204 million worth of pollution from the air annually, and store 16.9 million tons of carbon valued at $350 million.

The statewide survey of Tennessee's urban forest is one of a series of pilot studies initiated to determine the structure, condition, and function of forests in urban areas at a broad scale, beyond just one city or community. The Tennessee study is the second pilot to incorporate the full panel of urban plots throughout the State.

Table 1—Summary of urban forest population estimates, Tennessee, 2005–09

Land use	Area	Trees	Three most common species					
			1		2		3	
	acres	*number*		*%*		*%*		*%*
Forest	233,742	160,154,000	Chinese privet	11.6	Eastern redcedar	6.4	American beech	5.3
Transportation	397,362	44,171,000	Virginia pine	18.3	Flowering dogwood	10.1	Eastern redcedar	8.2
Residential	366,197	37,599,000	Virginia pine	13.0	Amur honeysuckle	11.7	Flowering dogwood	10.4
Other urban	210,369	21,778,000	Chinese privet	22.3	Flowering dogwood	10.7	Tree-of-heaven	8.5
Agriculture	186,993	14,189,000	Hackberry	29.0	Winged elm	14.1	Eastern redcedar	10.3
Commercial/industrial	163,620	6,225,000	Hawthorn	25.0	Mimosa	16.3	Sweetgum	9.4
Total urban	1,558,282	284,116,000	Chinese privet[a]	10.4	Virginia pine[a]	6.0	Eastern redcedar[a]	6.0

1, 2, and 3 = first-, second-, and third-most common tree within each land use, respectively.

[a] 1, 2, and 3 = first-, second-, and third-most common tree for all urban trees, respectively.

Introduction

Urban vegetation, particularly trees, provides numerous benefits that can improve environmental quality and human health in and around urban areas. Urban trees in particular make significant contributions to improve air and water quality, reduce energy used for heating and cooling buildings, cool air temperatures, reduce ultraviolet radiation, and many other environmental and social benefits (Nowak and Dwyer 2007). Structural data about these trees and forests (e.g., number of trees, species composition, tree size, health, and tree location) provide the basis to estimate numerous ecosystem services and values derived from these natural resources and establish the foundation to improve management to enhance these services for future generations.

Urban forests are comprised of all trees (both within and outside forested stands) that occur within the U.S. Census Bureau definition of urban areas. Urban areas are defined as all territory, population, and housing units located within urbanized areas or urban clusters, which are based on population density (areas with core population density of 1,000 people per square mile), but includes surrounding areas with lesser population density (see U.S. Department of Commerce 2007 for definitions) (fig. 1).

Forests that are measured by the U.S. Department of Agriculture (USDA) Forest Service, Forest Inventory and Analysis (FIA) program are defined as areas at least 1 acre in size, at least 120 feet wide, and at least 10 percent stocked. Forested plots must also have an understory that is undisturbed by another land use (U.S. Department of Agriculture 2010). FIA-defined forests cover the entire State (fig. 2) and exist within urban forests. The areas of overlap in urban areas are referred to as "forests within urban areas" and are subset of the entire urban forest (fig. 3).

Urban forests provide a multitude of benefits to society, such as recreational opportunities, aesthetics, and cleaner air and water. Millions of dollars are spent annually to maintain them, yet relatively little is known about this important resource. In an attempt to learn more about this resource and to aid in its management and planning, a pilot study to apply a national Forest Health Monitoring (FHM) protocol within urban areas was conducted. Based on standard USDA Forest Service FHM and FIA field sampling protocols, the national plot inventory grid was used to sample urban areas within the State of Tennessee. The pilot study was developed to test the feasibility of various procedures and analysis techniques to be used in urban forest resource monitoring. Similar pilot studies were and are being conducted in Indiana (2001) (Nowak and others 2007), Wisconsin (2002) (Cumming and others 2007), New Jersey (2003–04), and Colorado (2005–09).

Management of any natural resource requires knowledge of type, size, and quantity of the resource. Inventories and assessments to monitor

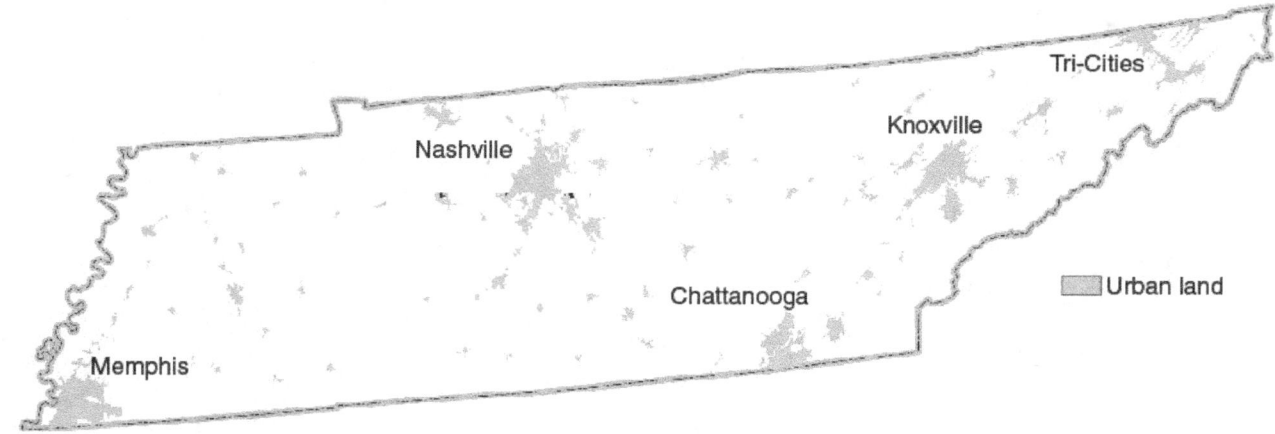

Figure 1—Urban land area in Tennessee. Trees with these urban areas are part of the urban forest, 2000.

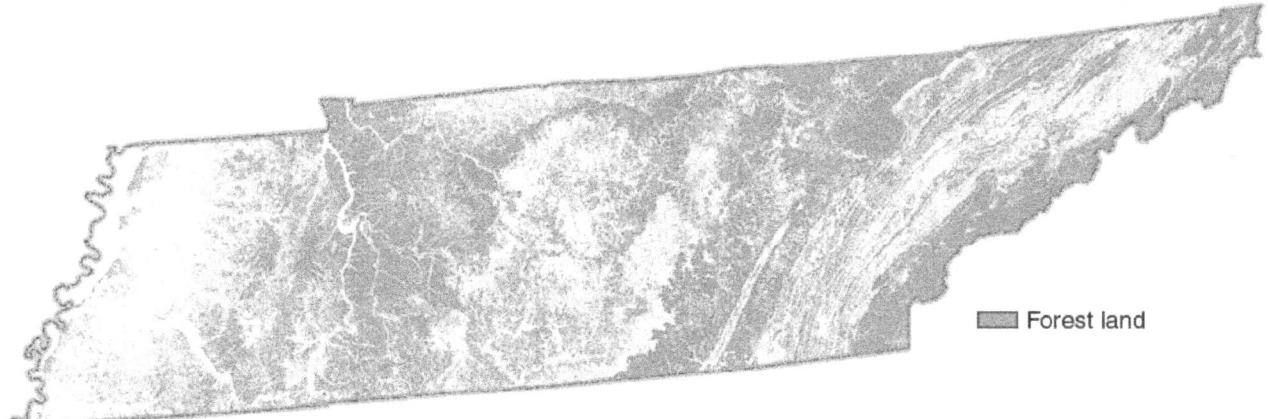

Figure 2—Forest land in Tennessee, 2000.

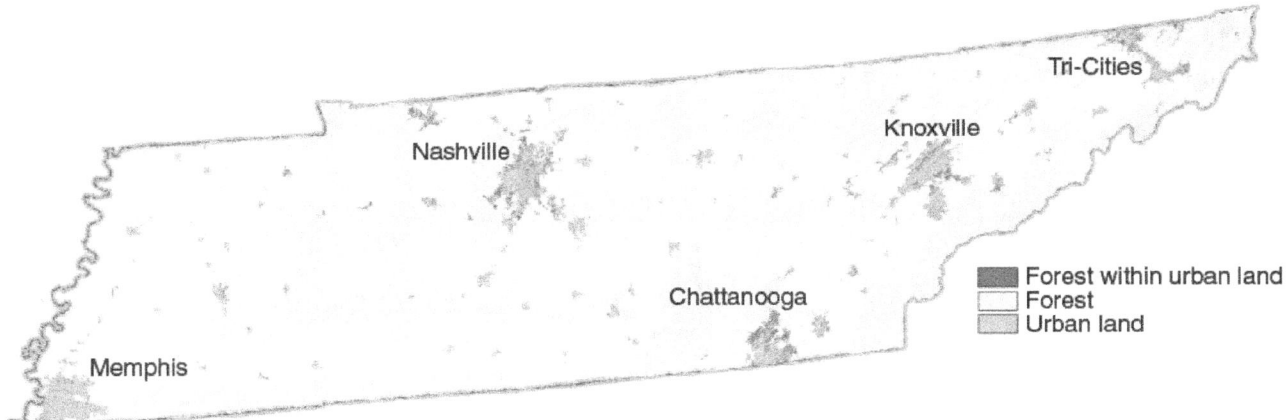

Figure 3—Overlap between forest land and urban land. Dark green areas of overlap are referred to as "forests within urban areas," Tennessee, 2000.

composition, size, and health provide information about the current status of urban forests, and, if compiled periodically, information about how the forest changes over time. The current study is the first statewide inventory and FHM effort to quantify the urban forests within the State of Tennessee. Data from 255 field plots located throughout urban Tennessee were analyzed using the i-Tree Eco model to quantify the State's urban forest structure, health, benefits, and values (Nowak and others 2008). Field crews visited the plots during the summers of 2005–09, sampling about one-fifth of plots each year.

If the pilot protocol were to be implemented into a regular inventory and assessment, resource managers would be able to monitor how urban forests change over time due to urbanization pressures, management techniques, and the influence of stressors, such as invasive pests or extreme weather events. In addition, information could be compiled on which species perform the best under differing urban conditions and how long various species live on average in urban areas.

This report details information on: a) the extent and distribution of the urban forest, b) the characteristics of the urban tree population, c) the health of the urban trees, and d) ecosystem services and values provided by the urban trees. Methods used in gathering these data are given in appendix A.

Extent and Land Use Distribution of Tennessee's Urban Forest

The 2000 census-defined urban land area used in this study is about 5.8 percent of the total land area of Tennessee, an increase from 4.4 percent in 1990 (fig. 1). Tennessee currently ranks 19th in the coterminous United States for amount of urban land and 14th in percent urban growth between 1990 and 2000 (Nowak and others 2005). Forecasts predict urban land in the State will grow from 5.8 percent in 2000 to 15.3 percent of the land area by 2050, advancing Tennessee to 15th in the State ranking of percent urban land (Nowak and Walton 2005). Urban land area is, of course, influenced by human population. State population was 4.88 million in 1990 and increased to 5.69 million in 2000 and 6.35 million in 2010 (U.S. Department of Commerce 2011a). Tennessee's population is projected to continue to increase between 2000 and 2030 by 29.7 percent or 1.7 million people to 7.38 million in 2030 (U.S. Department of Commerce 2011b).

There were a total of 1.6 million acres of urban areas in the State of Tennessee in 2000, of which 233,742 acres were forest (table 2). Urban areas were classified by their principal land use. The land uses designated for this study were residential, commercial/industrial, transportation (highways, rights-of-way, etc.), agriculture, forests (undeveloped tree covered areas within the urban boundaries), and other urban. Examples of other urban include cemeteries, parks, golf courses, institutional land, and nonforest open space. The predominant urban land uses are

transportation (25 percent), followed by residential (24 percent), forest (15 percent), other (13 percent), agriculture (12 percent), and commercial/industrial (11 percent) (fig. 4).

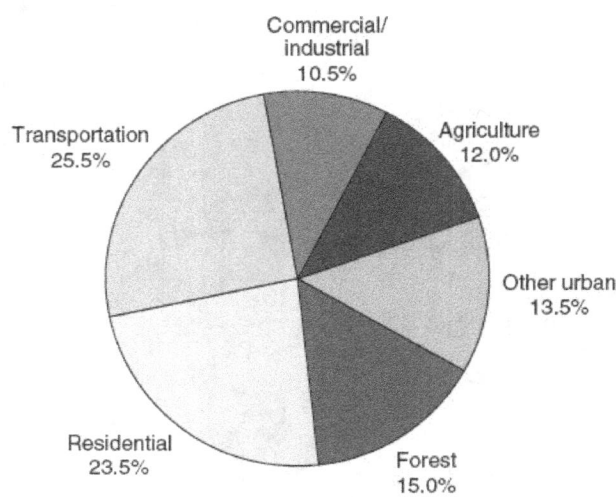

Figure 4—Land distribution based on urban plots, Tennessee, 2005–09.

In comparison, forest land outside of the urban boundary in Tennessee has remained about one-half of the land base in the State since the early 1960s. There were 13.7 million acres of forest in Tennessee according to the 1961 survey and 13.8 million acres in 2004 (Oswalt and others 2009). In 2009, it is estimated that all forest land accounts for 14 million acres.[1]

There are an estimated 284.1 million trees in Tennessee's urban areas (as a comparison, there are about 8 billion trees on forest land outside urban areas across the State). Of these urban trees, about 160.2 million (56.3 percent) are found in forest land use.

There were a total of 2,418 trees sampled. The average diameter at breast height (d.b.h.) was 4.2 inches. The average basal area (cross sectional area of a tree at 4.5 feet, expressed as square feet per acre) was 41.9.

---

[1] Unpublished data on file with: Christopher M. Oswalt, Research Forester, Southern Research Station, 4700 Old Kingston Pike, Knoxville, TN 37919.

Table 2—Area of land within urban areas by land use, Tennessee, 2005–09

Land use	Area
	acres
Transportation	397,362
Residential	366,197
Forest	233,742
Other urban	210,369
Agriculture	186,993
Commercial/industrial	163,620
Total urban	1,558,282

The average number of trees per acre in Tennessee urban areas was 182.3 (table 3, fig. 5). Tree density within the urban boundary was highest on forest land (685 trees per acre), followed by transportation lands (111 trees per acre) and other urban land (104 trees per acre). Land uses with trees having the highest average d.b.h. were residential (5.5 inches), other (5.0 inches), and agriculture (4.4 inches). The highest average basal areas per acre were found on forest land (129.4 square feet per acre), residential land (38.1 square feet per acre), and other (29.4 square feet per acre).

Table 3—Forest and tree characteristics by land use type, Tennessee, 2005–09

Land use	Urban land	Trees		Basal area	D.b.h.	
					Average	Median
	percent	million	trees/ acre	ft²/ac	- - - - inches - - - -	
Transportation	25.5	44.2	111.2	25.6	4.3	2.8
Residential	23.5	37.6	102.7	38.1	5.5	3.2
Forest	15.0	160.2	685.2	129.4	3.8	2.3
Other	13.5	21.8	103.5	29.4	5.0	3.2
Agriculture	12.0	14.2	75.9	16.6	4.4	3.0
Commercial/industrial	10.5	6.2	38.0	9.6	4.1	2.1
Total urban	100.0	284.1	182.3	41.9	4.2	2.6

D.b.h. = Diameter at breast height.

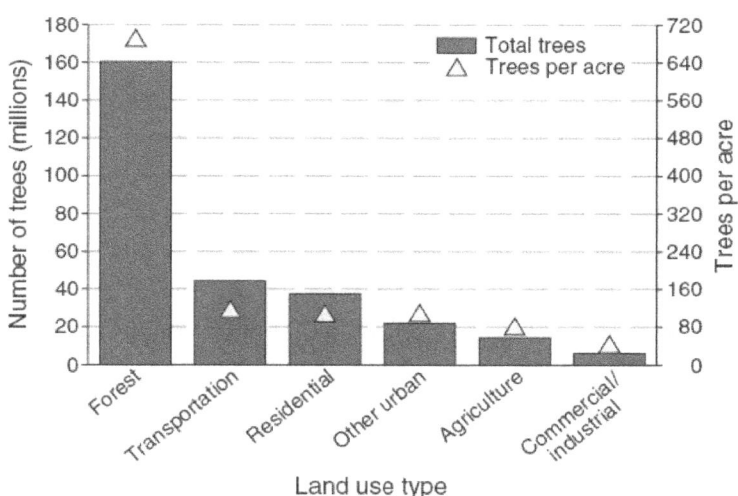

Figure 5—Tree population and density by land use type, Tennessee, 2005–09.

Common Trees of Tennessee's Forests

A comparison of the most common trees found in urban areas within Tennessee with the most common trees found in all forests statewide illustrates the differences that exist among the different forests. Many unfamiliar and even nonnative invasive species can be commonly found within the urban boundary and these areas can maintain large tree populations. For example, based simply on number of stems, Chinese privet is the most common species found within Tennessee's urban areas. However, red maple was the most common species in terms of number of individual stems recorded on forest land and was estimated to account for nearly 10 percent of the statewide population of all-live stems across the State (sidebar fig. 1). It is important to note, however, that all oak species combined comprise a very substantial proportion of the total estimated number of stems. While >100 distinct species were sampled across the State, the top 20 species account for about 75 percent of all-live trees. In addition to having large populations in Tennessee, red maple, sugar maple, and yellow-poplar are some of the most widely distributed tree species in the State as well. The tree species that account for the greatest carbon accumulation, generally regarded as the most dominant, are white oak, chestnut oak, and yellow-poplar (sidebar fig. 2).

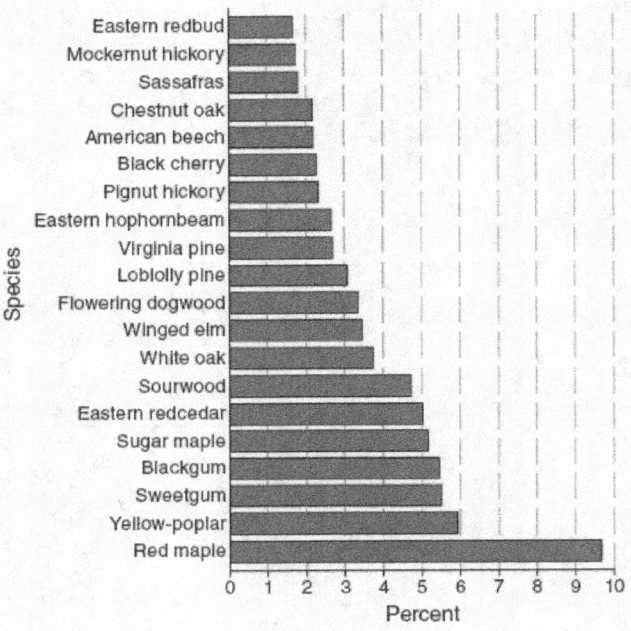

Sidebar figure 1—Twenty most common trees according to the percent of total number of trees on all forest land in Tennessee, 2009.

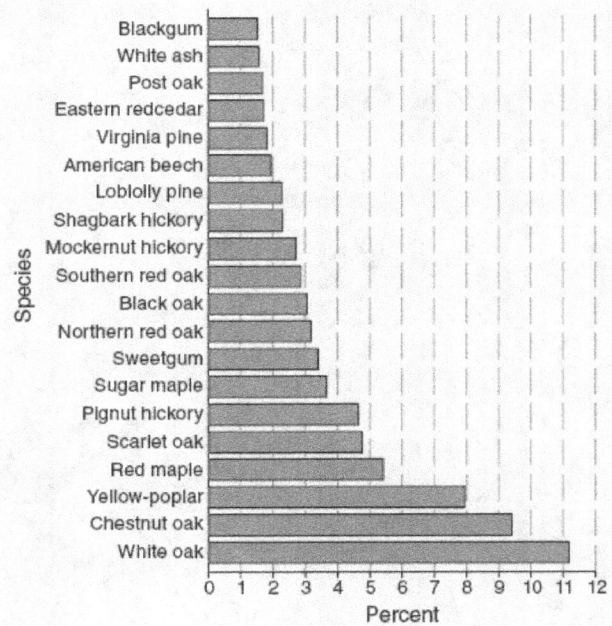

Sidebar figure 2—Twenty most common trees according to the percent of total carbon stored on all forest land in Tennessee, 2009.

The Tree Population and Species Characteristics of Tennessee's Urban Forest

Species Composition

The most common species observed in Tennessee urban areas as a percent of the total urban tree population were Chinese privet (10.6 percent), Virginia pine (6.0 percent), and eastern redcedar (6.0 percent) (fig. 6). By comparison, the most common tree species found statewide are red maple, yellow-poplar (the State tree), and sweetgum. The 10 most frequent species account for 49.8 percent of the total urban tree population. Similarly, statewide the 10 most frequent species account for 52 percent of all trees found in Tennessee forests outside the urban boundary.

The distribution of the top 10 species in urban areas varied by land use (fig. 7). The greatest proportion of many of the top 10 species is found in urban forested lands. For example, almost all of the American beech trees were found on urban forested land uses. Also, various species tended to be more dominant in certain land uses (fig. 8). For example, hackberry comprises about 30 percent of the agricultural tree population, while Chinese privet comprises >20 percent of the other urban land use. Species composition also varied by tree size. For trees ≤5 inches d.b.h. (trees measured on microplots), the common species were Chinese privet (13.7 percent), Virginia pine (6.3 percent), and flowering dogwood (6.1 percent) (fig. 9). For trees >5 inches d.b.h., the common species were eastern redcedar (6.6 percent), hackberry (6.2 percent), and Virginia pine (5.2 percent) (fig. 10). A total of 99 species were encountered within urban forests whereas 119 were encountered on all forest land across the State (Oswalt and others 2009). The scientific names of the species sampled are found in appendix B. Total species summary information is provided in appendix C.

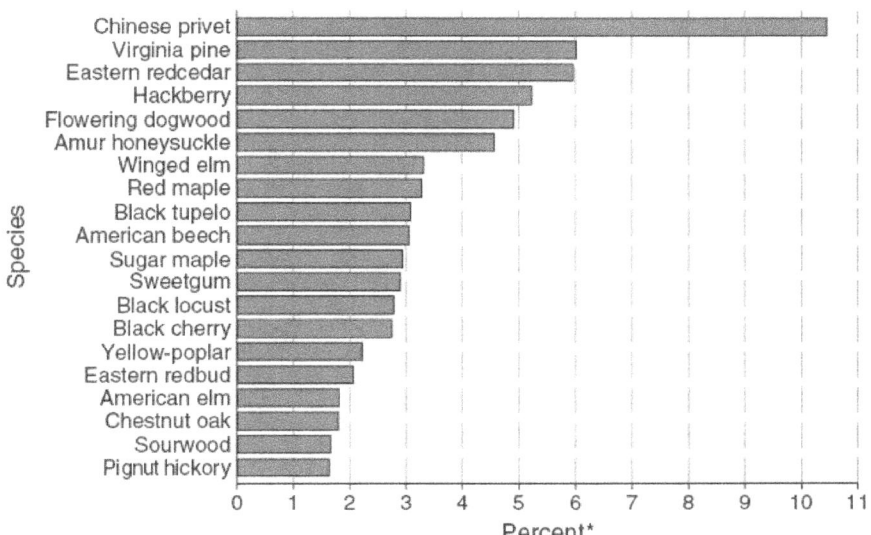

*Other 73 species = 27.6 percent.

Figure 6—Percent of total urban tree population for 20 most common tree species, Tennessee, 2005–09.

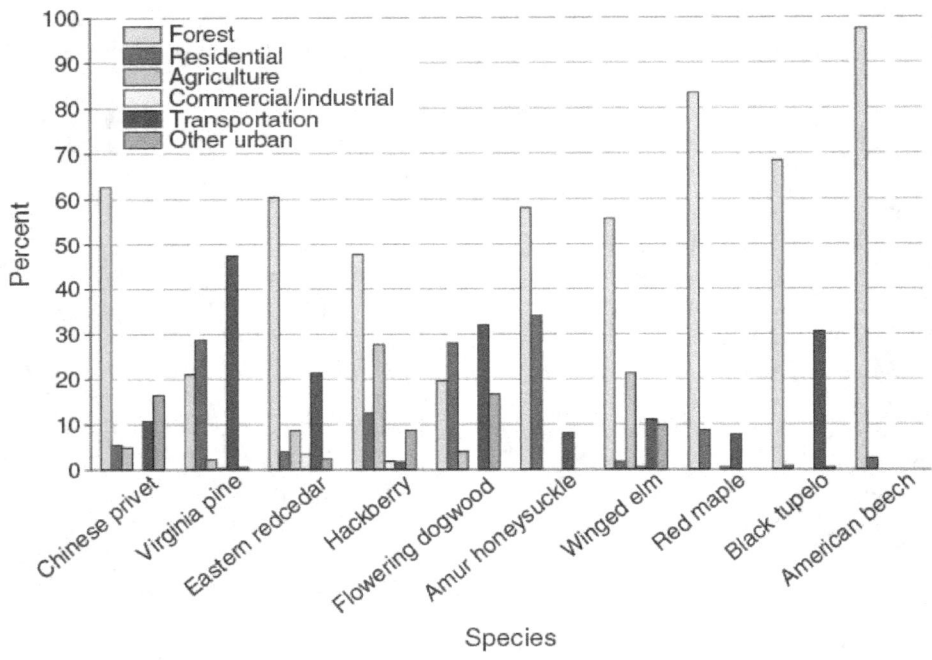

Figure 7—Distribution (percent of species population) of top 10 species by land use type. For example, 63 percent of Chinese privet is found in forests, Tennessee, 2005–09.

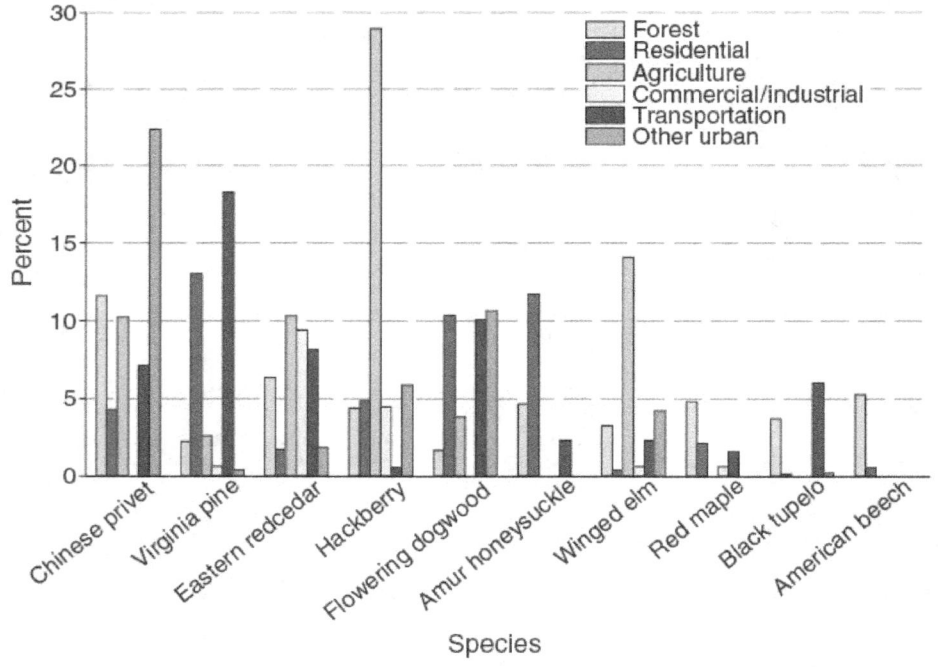

Figure 8—Percent of land use occupied by top 10 tree species. For example, 12 percent of forest trees are Chinese privet, Tennessee, 2005–09.

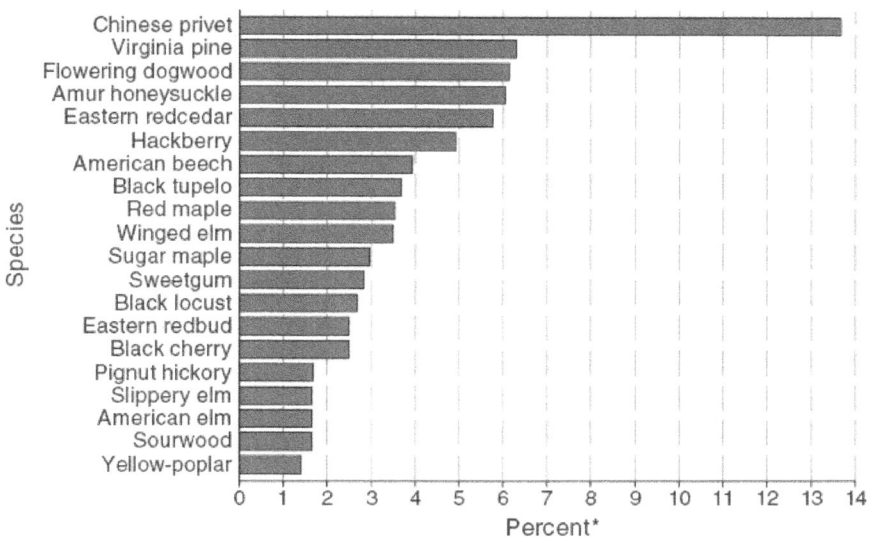

*Other 38 species = 21.0 percent.

Figure 9—Percent of total urban tree population ≤5 inches diameter at breast height (d.b.h.) for 20 most common species ≤5 inches d.b.h., Tennessee, 2005–09.

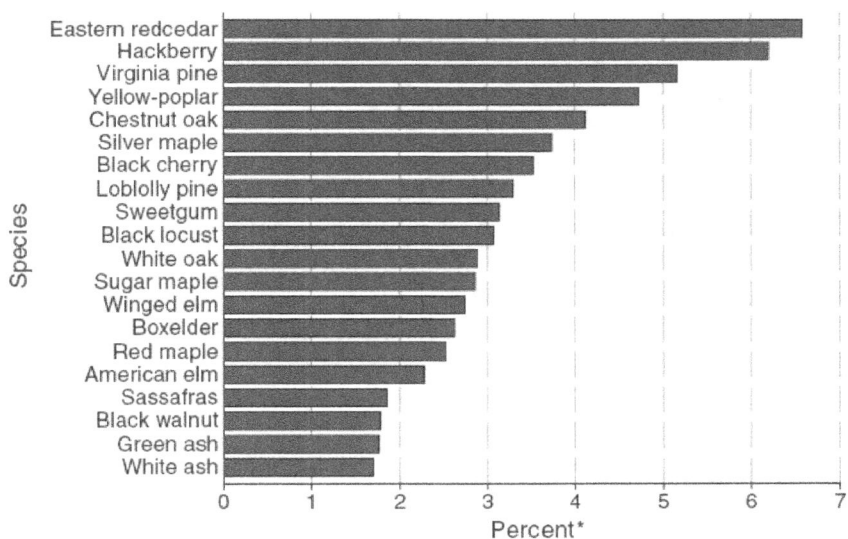

*Other 74 species = 33.5 percent.

Figure 10—Percent of total urban tree population >5 inches diameter at breast height (d.b.h.) for 20 most common species >5 inches d.b.h., Tennessee, 2005–09.

Species composition varies by land use. The most common species on transportation lands were Virginia pine (18.3 percent), flowering dogwood (10.1 percent), and eastern redcedar (8.2 percent) (fig. 11). The most common species on residential lands were Virginia pine (13.0 percent), Amur honeysuckle (11.7 percent), and flowering dogwood (10.4 percent) (fig. 12). The most common species

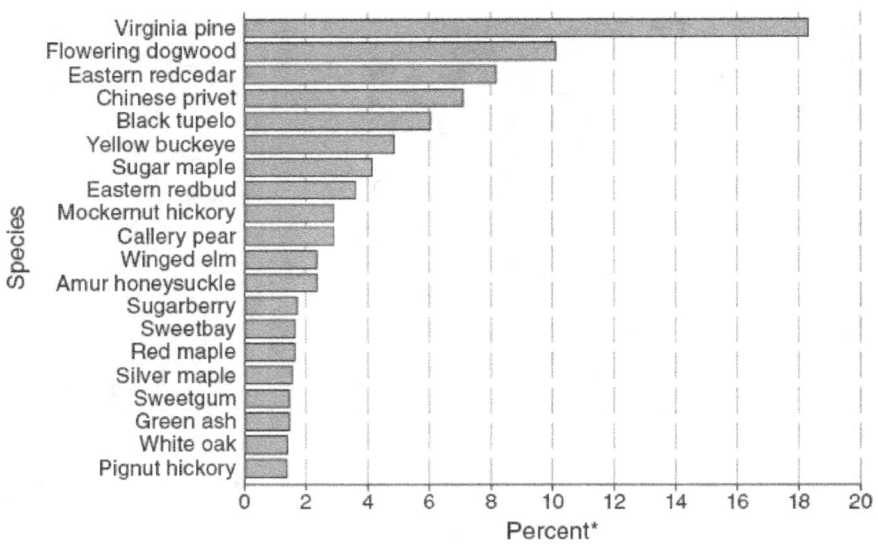

*Other 38 species = 15.0 percent.

Figure 11—Percent of total transportation tree population for 20 most common tree species in transportation land use, Tennessee, 2005–09.

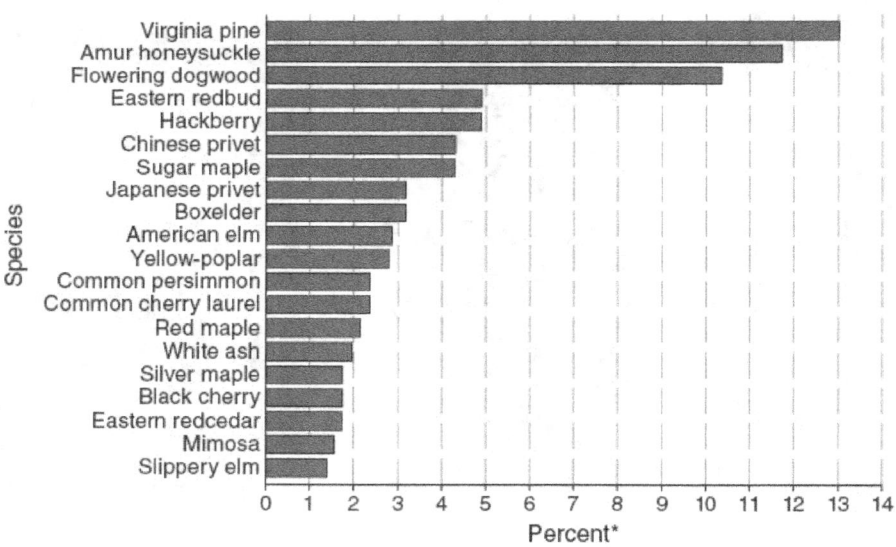

*Other 49 species = 17.5 percent.

Figure 12—Percent of total residential tree population for 20 most common tree species in residential land use, Tennessee, 2005–09.

on forest lands were Chinese privet (11.6 percent), eastern redcedar (6.4 percent), and American beech (5.3 percent) (fig. 13). The most common species on other lands were Chinese privet (22.3 percent), flowering dogwood (10.7 percent), and tree-of-heaven (8.5 percent) (fig. 14). The most common species on agricultural lands were hackberry (29.0 percent), winged elm (14.1 percent), and eastern redcedar

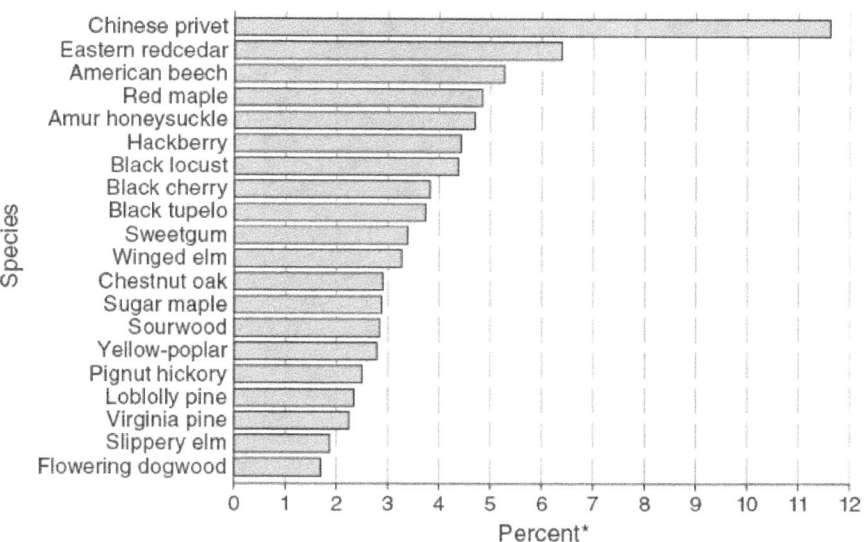

*Other 54 species = 22.1 percent.

Figure 13—Percent of total forest tree population for 20 most common tree species in forest land use, Tennessee, 2005–09.

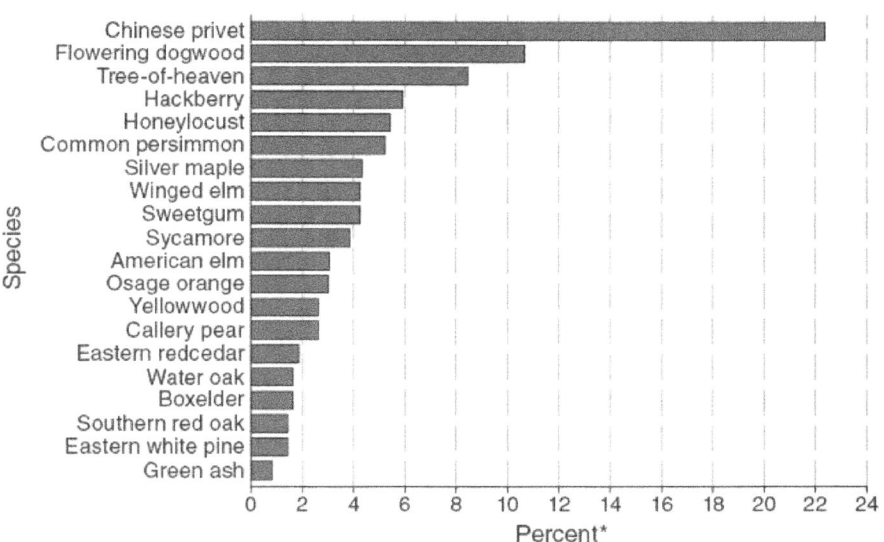

*Other 15 species = 5.1 percent.

Figure 14—Percent of total "other" tree population for 20 most common tree species in other land use, Tennessee, 2005–09.

(10.3 percent) (fig. 15). The most common species on commercial/industrial lands were hawthorn (25.0 percent), mimosa (16.3 percent), and sweetgum (9.4 percent) (fig. 16). Total species summary information by land use type is provided in appendix D.

Urban forests are a mix of native tree species that existed prior to the development of the city and exotic species that were introduced by residents or other means. Thus, urban forests often have a tree diversity that is higher than surrounding native

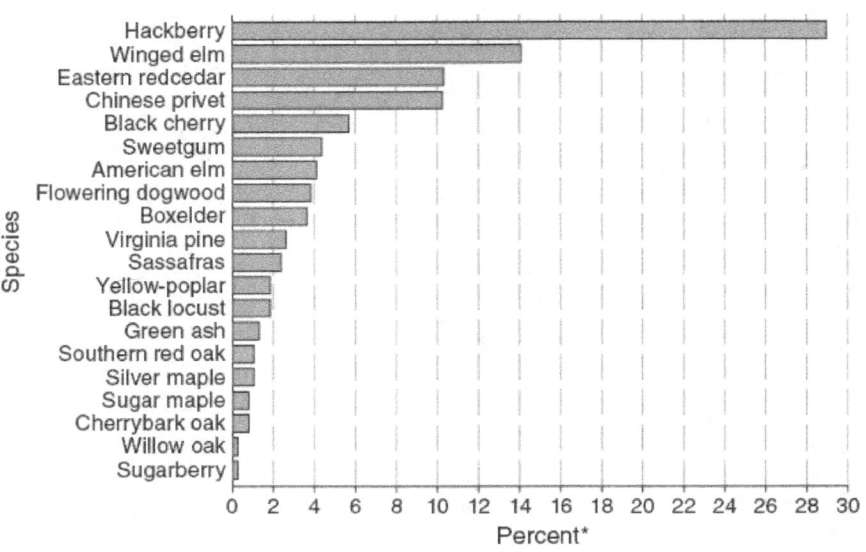

*Other 2 species = 0.5 percent.

Figure 15—Percent of total agricultural tree population for 20 most common tree species in agricultural land use, Tennessee, 2005–09.

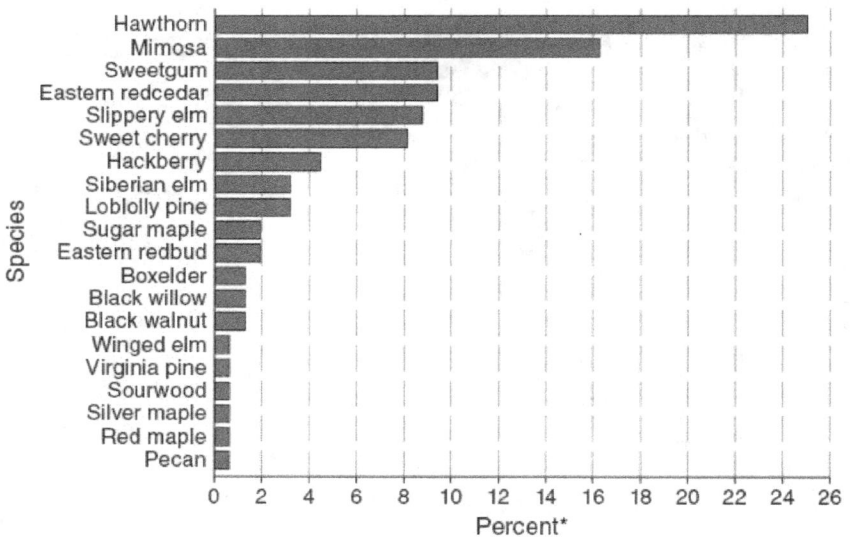

*Other species (cherry) = 0.6 percent.

Figure 16—Percent of total commercial/industrial tree population for 20 most common tree species in commercial/industrial land use, Tennessee, 2005–09.

landscapes. Increased tree diversity can minimize the overall impact or destruction by a species-specific insect or disease, but the increase in the number of exotic plants can also pose a risk to native plants if some of the exotic species are invasive plants that can potentially out-compete and displace native species.

Species native to North America comprise 85 percent of trees in urban areas in Tennessee, while 71 percent are native to Tennessee specifically. Most exotic species identified originated from Asia (13.6 percent) (fig. 17).

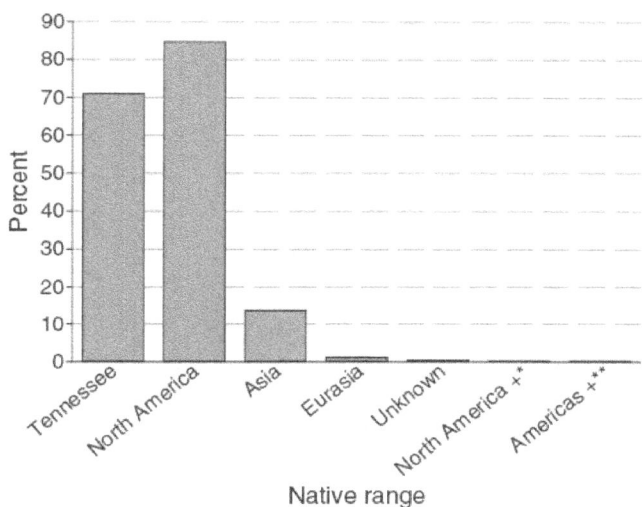

* Native to North America and one other continent, excluding South America.
** Native to North and South America, and one other continent.

Figure 17—Native range distribution of urban trees in Tennessee, 2009.

A total of 120 different species have recently been observed on forested plots across the State, including those forested plots within the urban boundary. The most frequent species statewide differ slightly from those found on forests within the urban boundary. Red maple is the most common tree found in Tennessee across all forest land in the State (sidebar fig. 1), followed by yellow-poplar, sweetgum, and blackgum. On forest land within the urban boundary Chinese privet (an invasive), eastern redcedar, and American beech are more common than red maple. Moreover, yellow-poplar, the State tree, is only the 15th most commonly found tree on forest land within the urban boundary, while it is the second most common tree statewide. White oak is the tree species with the most stored carbon (sidebar fig. 2) indicating that while red maple is more common in number of trees, white oak trees tend to be larger on average. Chestnut oak and yellow-poplar also have more stored carbon on forest land in Tennessee than red maple. Virginia pine, while the most commonly found tree on residential and transportation land within the urban boundary is the 12th most common tree on forest land statewide.

Tree Size Distribution

Tree stem diameter is used to estimate wood volume and mass. Unlike commercial forestry, where trees are harvested as a crop and volumes are used to estimate amount of timber products, urban wood volume can be translated into tons of carbon stored or carbon sequestered per year. As States and local units of government become more interested in environmental services provided by "green infrastructure," estimates of carbon storage and sequestration rates by trees will become increasingly more important.

That is not to say, however, that urban wood is not a commodity in its own right. Development of technologies, like portable saw mills, and increasing demand for specialty woods are making it more common for cities and local governments to market urban wood that is scheduled for removals as a timber product, rather than disposing as a wood waste or processing for mulch. In this case, knowledge of wood volumes for marketing plans and management is crucial (Bratkovich 2001). Thus, estimates of urban tree mass can provide information related to wood used for timber products or the amount of waste wood that may have to be disposed. In addition to basal area, tree leaf surface area is an important measure for determining the species effects on many ecosystem services (e.g., air temperature cooling, pollution removal) as many services are directly related to leaf surface area.

Tree diameter measurements are used by managers when creating plans for tree maintenance, removals, and planting. When coupled with species information, size estimates can assist managers to determine long-term patterns of tree survival, selection, and replacement (Cumming and others 2001).

Species that dominate Tennessee's urban land in terms of overall basal area are yellow-poplar, chestnut oak, and white oak (table 4). These tree species are the same species that dominate all forest land in Tennessee (see sidebar fig. 2), which is a potential indication of the dominant effect of remnant stands or natural forest ecosystem processes in urban areas in Tennessee.

Trees that dominate in terms of leaf surface area are hackberry (6.9 percent of total leaf surface area), yellow-poplar (5.4 percent), flowering dogwood (4.5 percent), and eastern redcedar (4.5 percent)

Table 4—Top 20 urban tree species in terms of basal area, Tennessee, 2005–09

Species	Population	Basal area		D.b.h. Average	D.b.h. Median
	percent	*ft²/ac*	*percent*	*- - - - inches - - - -*	
Yellow-poplar	2.2	2.8	6.8	7.9	5.0
Chestnut oak	1.8	2.6	6.1	9.3	8.0
White oak	1.0	2.1	5.0	10.7	7.1
Virginia pine	6.0	1.9	4.6	3.8	2.3
Hackberry	5.2	1.9	4.6	4.4	3.0
Eastern redcedar	6.0	1.7	4.1	4.0	3.3
Silver maple	1.2	1.5	3.5	8.7	7.1
Sweetgum	2.9	1.3	3.1	4.3	2.2
Southern red oak	0.7	1.2	3.0	9.4	7.0
Red maple	3.3	1.2	2.9	4.1	3.3
Sugar maple	2.9	1.0	2.5	4.6	4.5
Loblolly pine	1.6	1.0	2.4	6.0	5.0
Black cherry	2.7	1.0	2.4	4.5	4.4
Boxelder	1.4	0.8	2.0	5.5	2.1
White ash	0.7	0.7	1.7	7.6	6.0
Flowering dogwood	4.9	0.7	1.7	3.1	2.2
Black locust	2.8	0.7	1.7	3.5	1.0
Water oak	0.2	0.7	1.7	16.8	12.0
Chinese privet	10.4	0.7	1.7	1.9	1.3
Black oak	0.4	0.7	1.7	11.7	9.0

D.b.h. = Diameter at breast height.

(fig. 18). Leaf area estimates are likely a better indication of ecosystem services derived from trees than basal area as the leaf area estimates are directly related to the parts of the trees where most of the services are derived.

Tree diameter distribution information provides information related to tree size distribution and approximate age distribution, which are important for understanding population dynamics. For example, for a sustainable population, more small trees are typically required than larger trees as the smaller tree population eventually will fill the larger diameter population classes through time. However, some small statured species (e.g., Chinese privet) will not attain a large diameter or stature. The diameter distribution for Tennessee's urban forest displays the typical inverse-J shape distribution (fig. 19). On a per tree basis, larger trees can provide more services, such as air pollution removal and storm water mitigation, than smaller trees.

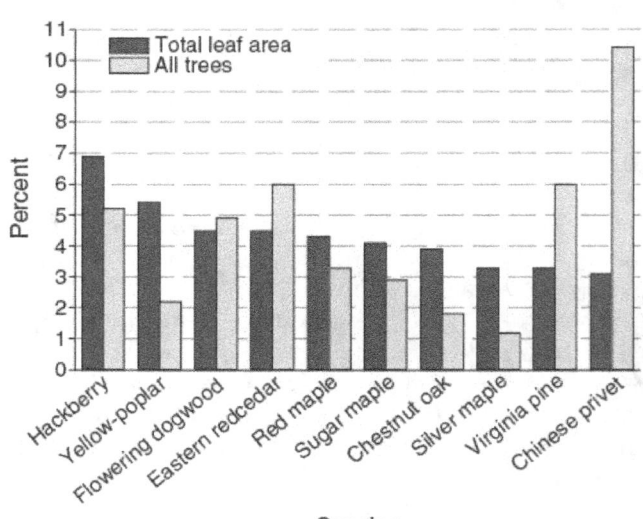

Figure 18—Percent of total leaf surface area for top 10 species in terms of leaf surface area, Tennessee, 2005–09. Percent leaf surface area is contrasted with percent of total number of trees in the urban population. Species with percent leaf area much greater than percent total population tend to be relatively large, healthy trees on average. Species with percent of total population much greater than percent total leaf area tend to be relatively small and/or unhealthy trees on average.

Of the 10 most common species, Chinese privet, amur honeysuckle, and American beech are dominated by trees <4 inches d.b.h. (fig. 20). The top 10 species with the largest average diameters were hackberry, red maple, and eastern redcedar. Diameter distribution patterns among the land use classes were similar, with trees in forests having the greatest proportion of trees <6 inches d.b.h. and trees in residential lands have the lowest proportion of small trees (fig. 21). Detailed statistics (e.g., average d.b.h. and basal area) on urban trees can be found in appendix B. Detailed tree statistics by land use type are given in appendix D.

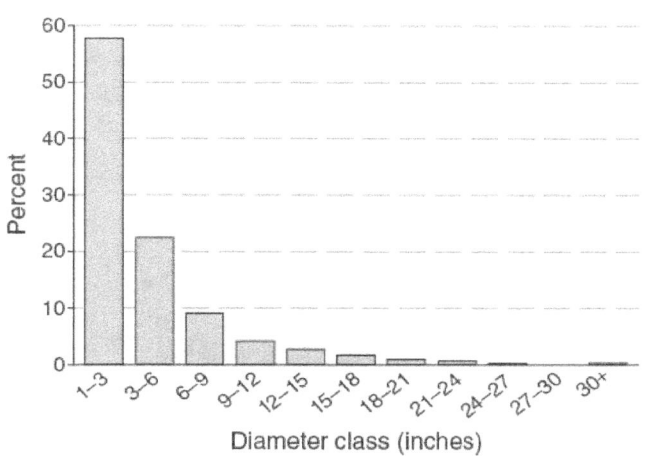

Figure 19—Proportion of urban tree population by diameter class, Tennessee, 2005–09.

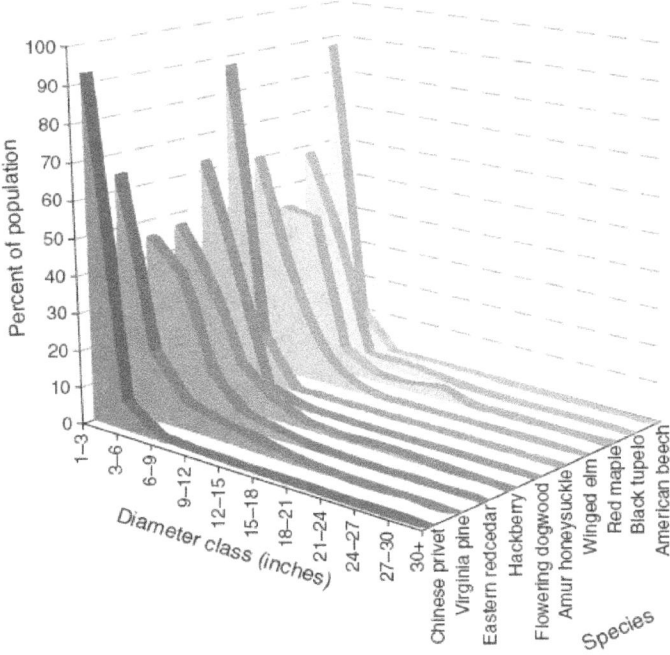

Figure 20—Proportion of top 10 species populations by diameter class, Tennessee, 2005–09.

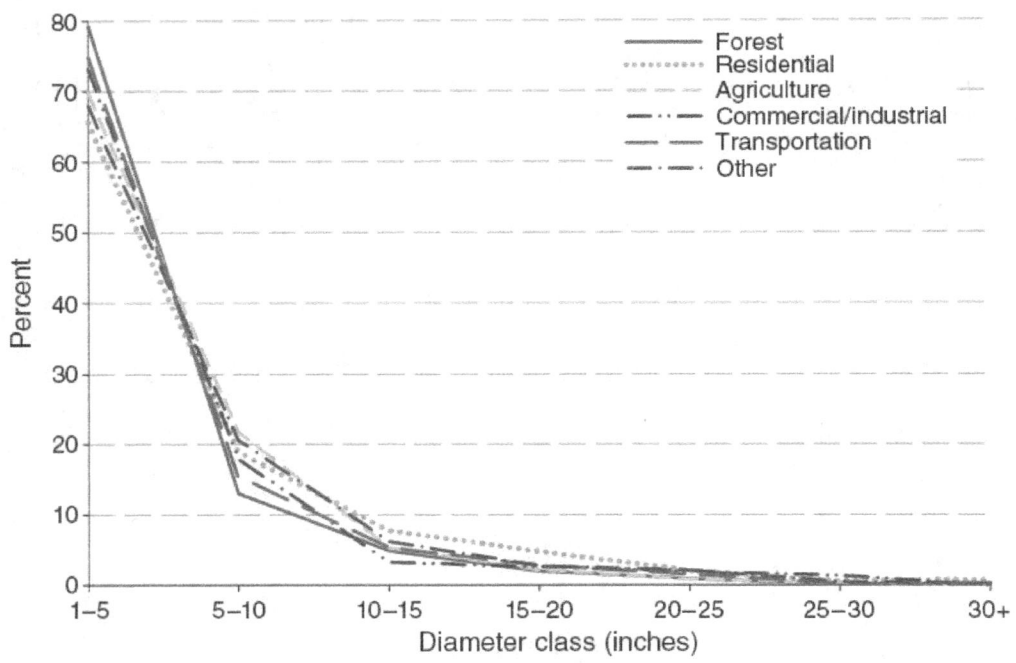

Figure 21—Diameter distribution by land use class, Tennessee, 2005–09.

Tree and Ground Cover

Tree cover in urban areas in Tennessee was interpreted using Google Earth imagery circa 2005. Five thousand points were randomly located within the urban areas of Tennessee. Some of the imagery was not interpretable due to cloud cover or poor image resolution (e.g., 30 m satellite imagery). A total of 3,914 points were interpreted as either tree/shrub cover, impervious surfaces (concrete, asphalt, etc.), water, or other. Urban tree cover in Tennessee is estimated at 37.7 percent (table 5).

The ground cover in urban Tennessee is dominated by herbaceous (grass and other nonwoody plants) cover

Table 5—Estimates of cover type in urban Tennessee, 2005		
Cover type	Percent	SE
Tree/shrub	37.7	0.8
Impervious	22.6	0.7
Water	1.1	0.2
Other	38.6	0.8

SE = standard error.

(56.7 percent) (fig. 22). Building cover was highest in commercial/industrial land uses (16.1 percent), impervious cover (excluding buildings) was highest in transportation land uses (29.6 percent), herbaceous cover was highest in agricultural lands (87.5 percent), and duff/mulch cover was highest in forest lands (50 percent).

Trees in Maintained and Nonmaintained Urban Areas

Each tree was classified as to whether it was found in a maintained or nonmaintained area. Maintained areas are defined as those which are regularly impacted by mowing, weeding, herbicide applications, etc. Trees found in a maintained area does not imply each tree had maintenance. The maintained and nonmaintained classification was added to the site description to distinguish "woodlot"-like areas sampled during the study. Examples of maintained areas include lawns, rights-of-way, and parks. Whether a tree was growing in a maintained vs. nonmaintained area was only noted from 2006 to 2009 (4 years). Overall, 9.4 percent of the trees (26.5 million) were classified as growing in maintained areas. Land uses with the highest proportion of trees in maintained areas were agriculture, residential,

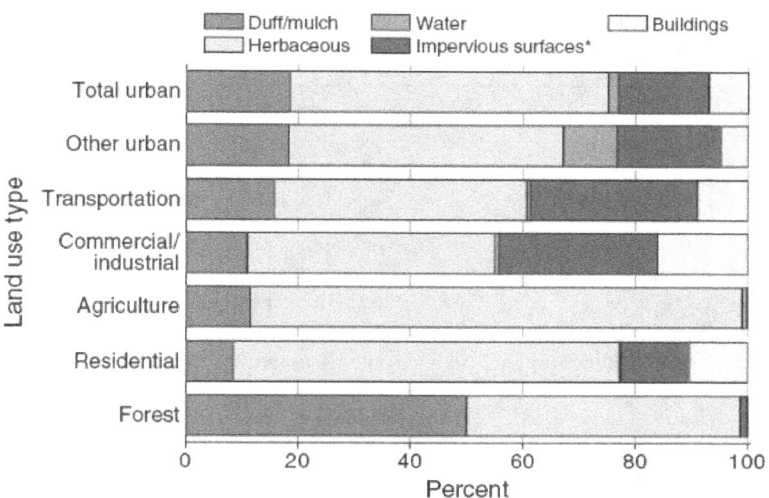

*Excluding buildings.

Figure 22—Ground cover distribution by land use type and for entire urban area, Tennessee, 2005–09.

and commercial/industrial (table 6). Species with the highest proportion of its population in maintained areas were eastern white pine, pecan, and silver maple (table 7). Of the maintained tree population, the most common species were flowering dogwood (18.9 percent), hackberry (18.6 percent), and Chinese privet (12.2 percent) (table 8). The preponderance of Chinese privet within maintained areas may be an indication of how this species is escaping to urban forest and other urban lands. Trees in maintained areas have a higher proportion of larger diameter trees than trees in nonmaintained areas (fig. 23).

Table 6—Percent of trees growing in maintained areas by land use, Tennessee, 2005–09

Land use	Trees
	percent
Agriculture	30.7
Residential	30.0
Commercial/industrial	21.8
Transportation	16.3
Other urban	10.7
Forest	0.0
Total	9.4

Table 7—Percent of trees in maintained areas (minimum sample size = 10) by species, Tennessee, 2005–09

Species	Trees	Species	Trees
	percent		*percent*
Eastern white pine	77.2	Sugarberry	4.0
Pecan	67.5	Eastern redcedar	3.9
Silver maple	54.9	Black oak	3.8
Callery pear	41.5	Yellow-poplar	3.1
Other species	41.2	Amur honeysuckle	3.1
Flowering dogwood	35.4	Sweetgum	2.2
Baldcypress	33.8	Black locust	2.1
Hackberry	33.5	Common persimmon	1.6
Water oak	23.6	Virginia pine	1.5
Cherrybark oak	20.8	Tree-of-heaven	1.5
Black walnut	17.0	American elm	1.3
Northern red oak	13.3	Sourwood	1.1
Chinese privet	10.9	Black cherry	0.9
Boxelder	10.5	Black tupelo	0.6
Eastern redbud	9.8	Chestnut oak	0.0
Sycamore	9.2	Winged elm	0.0
Post oak	9.1	Sassafras	0.0
White ash	9.1	Pignut hickory	0.0
Loblolly pine	7.5	Green ash	0.0
Chinkapin oak	7.1	Mockernut hickory	0.0
Shortleaf pine	6.2	American beech	0.0
Sugar maple	5.3	Shagbark hickory	0.0
White oak	5.0	Osage orange	0.0
Red maple	4.9	Slippery elm	0.0
Southern red oak	4.6	Bitternut hickory	0.0
Mimosa	4.2		

Table 8—Species composition (percent of all-live trees) in maintained areas, Tennessee, 2005–09

Species	Trees	Species	Trees	Species	Trees	Species	Trees
	percent		*percent*		*percent*		*percent*
Flowering dogwood	18.9	Pecan	1.3	Crabapple	0.4	Black cherry	0.3
Hackberry	18.6	Other species	1.2	Red mulberry	0.4	Chinkapin oak	0.3
Chinese privet	12.2	Virginia pine	1.0	Sycamore	0.4	Post oak	0.3
Silver maple	5.1	Southern magnolia	0.9	Common cherry laurel	0.4	Baldcypress	0.3
Callery pear	3.9	White ash	0.8	Northern pin oak	0.4	American elm	0.3
Sweetbay	3.0	Black walnut	0.8	Pin oak	0.4	Weeping willow	0.2
Eastern red cedar	2.4	Yellow-poplar	0.7	Cherrybark oak	0.4	Sourwood	0.2
Sweet cherry	2.2	Sweetgum	0.7	Black willow	0.4	Cherry	0.2
Eastern redbud	2.1	Eastern cottonwood	0.6	Scarlet oak	0.4	Black tupelo	0.2
Yellowwood	2.1	Black locust	0.6	Norway maple	0.3	Black oak	0.2
Sugar maple	1.7	White oak	0.6	Southern red oak	0.3	Tree-of-heaven	0.1
Red maple	1.7	Water oak	0.5	Willow oak	0.3	Common persimmon	0.1
Boxelder	1.6	Shortleaf pine	0.4	Northern red oak	0.3	Shumard oak	0.1
Amur honeysuckle	1.5	Southern crabapple	0.4	Mimosa	0.3	Northern white cedar	0.1
Eastern white pine	1.5	Elm	0.4	Chinese chestnut	0.3	Carolina hemlock	0.1
Loblolly pine	1.4	Sugarberry	0.4	American holly	0.3	Siberian elm	0.1

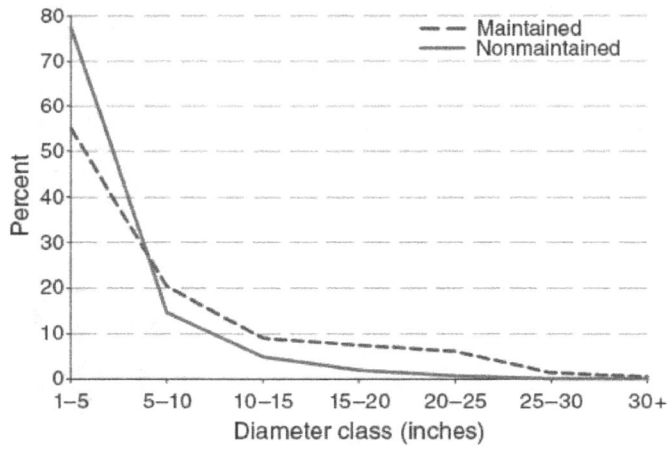

Figure 23—Diameter distribution of trees in maintained and nonmaintained areas, Tennessee, 2005–09.

Urban Forest Health

To evaluate tree condition, we used national FIA protocols for crown and damage ratings (Conklin and Byers 1992) for all trees ≥1 inch (see U.S. Department of Agriculture 2007 for details). Crown measurements evaluate the growth and vigor of the crown, as a whole, of each tree. Damage ratings describe symptoms on a tree where there are abnormalities in the visible roots, bark, branches, and leaves. Taken together, crown and damage ratings give an overall description of tree health. In addition to damage ratings, crews were asked to note the presence or absence of 44 different damages that can occur on trees in urban areas. These urban damage indicators are of specific interest to arborists and plant health specialists.

Tree Mortality

Overall, 1.8 percent of the total urban tree population was standing dead. Comparatively, 7.3 percent of trees >5 inches d.b.h. on nonurban forest land within the State are currently standing dead. The species with the highest percent of its total urban population in standing dead trees were pin cherry, serviceberry, sassafras, black locust, and black walnut (table 9). Interestingly, black locust is the third most numerous species with standing dead trees (53.0 percent) on forest land statewide. Across all forest land in the State, including within urban areas, fraser fir had the highest percent standing dead trees of all species at 90 percent. Other species with a higher percent of standing dead trees on all forest land include Table Mountain pine and Kentucky coffeetree with 59 and 51 percent of the species population as standing dead, respectively (Miles 2011).

Higher proportions of standing dead trees coupled with large tree populations may indicate potential insect, disease, or environmental problems associated with black locust, sassafras, and black walnut. Further evaluation and monitoring of these species is warranted. A high percent of dead trees does not necessarily indicate a health problem with the species, but could be due to the fact that some trees will naturally remain standing as dead trees for longer periods, or that they might be left standing dead depending upon the land use, risk associated with dead trees, and maintenance activities related to their removal. Thus, some species may have a higher proportion of dead trees as they are in locations where they are not immediately removed and therefore have a higher probability of being sampled as dead. Long-term monitoring of plots can help determine actual species mortality rates.

Land uses with the highest proportion of trees sampled as dead trees were commercial/industrial, forest, and agriculture (table 10).

Table 9—Species with the largest proportion of their total population classified as dead, Tennessee, 2005–09

Species	Population	Dead
	number	percent
Pin cherry	69,690	50.0
Serviceberry	75,493	46.2
Sassafras	2,656,708	17.3
Black locust	7,906,797	14.7
Black walnut	1,247,642	14.0
Shortleaf pine	1,634,528	12.8
Post oak	628,269	12.0
Scarlet oak	335,689	10.4
Black oak	1,165,417	9.5
Water oak	518,111	8.6

Table 10—Percent of tree population classified as dead by land use, Tennessee, 2005–09

Land use	Dead
	percent
Commercial/industrial	2.6
Forest	2.2
Agriculture	2.1
Residential	1.8
Transportation	1.0
Other urban	0.6

Crown Indicators of Forest Health

Measurement of tree crowns can be used as an indicator of tree health. Large dense crowns are often indicative of vigorously growing trees, while small, sparsely foliated crowns signal trees with little or no growth and possibly in a state of decline. Two measurements of crown health were used to estimate tree condition: dieback and density (table 11).

Crown dieback is demonstrative of tree health and is defined as recent mortality of small branches and twigs in the upper and outer portion of the trees' crown. Trees with crown dieback >25 percent may be in decline, for both hardwoods and conifers (Steinman 1998).

Crown density is an estimate of the crown condition of each tree relative to its potential, by determining the percentage of light blocked by branches and foliage. Crown density reflects gaps in the crown that may have been caused by declining tree health. For density estimates of both hardwoods and conifers, <30 percent generally indicate the tree is in poor health (Steinman 1998).

Dieback

Based on the live tree population with a minimum sample size of 20, species with highest percent crown dieback were black walnut, sassafras, and shagbark hickory (table 12). Black walnut, with an average percent dieback of 16.3 percent, may indicate a potential insect, disease, or environmental problem associated with this species and further evaluation is warranted. Due to the known presence of thousand cankers disease of black walnut in Tennessee (U.S. Department of Agriculture 2011), the observed dieback associated with this species justifies additional evaluation and monitoring. In this survey, black walnut was found on all land uses except agricultural.

Table 11—Average percent crown dieback, crown density, and percent of all-live trees for 20 most common species, Tennessee, 2005–09

| Species | Crown | | Population |
	Dieback	Density	
	percent		
Sourwood	7.1	26.7	1.7
Black cherry	5.0	34.7	2.7
Pignut hickory	4.3	30.3	1.6
Flowering dogwood	3.3	20.4	4.9
Black locust	3.3	14.5	2.8
Eastern redbud	3.0	16.9	2.1
Eastern redcedar	1.4	35.2	6.0
Hackberry	1.3	34.9	5.2
Yellow-poplar	1.3	38.2	2.2
Red maple	1.1	36.2	3.3
Sweetgum	1.0	39.1	2.9
Sugar maple	0.9	32.6	2.9
American elm	0.9	36.6	1.8
Chestnut oak	0.7	35.8	1.8
Chinese privet	0.5	10.9	10.4
Virginia pine	0.5	27.5	6.0
American beech	0.3	17.4	3.0
Winged elm	0.2	32.0	3.3
Black tupelo	0.2	23.5	3.1
Amur honeysuckle	0.0	2.8	4.6

Table 12—Species with highest average percent dieback (minimum sample size = 20), Tennessee, 2005–09

Species	Sample	Dieback
	number	percent
Black walnut	36	16.3
Sassafras	40	7.8
Shagbark hickory	27	7.1
Sourwood	41	7.1
Silver maple	70	6.9
Black cherry	83	5.0
Mockernut hickory	31	4.5
Pignut hickory	38	4.3
Osage orange	26	4.0
Slippery elm	25	3.5

Crown Density

Based on the live tree population with a minimum sample size of 20, species with lowest percent crown density were amur honeysuckle (2.8 percent), Chinese privet (10.9 percent), and black locust (14.5 percent) (table 13).

Table 13—Species with lowest average crown density (minimum sample size = 20), Tennessee, 2005–09

Species	Sample	Crown density
	number	*percent*
Amur honeysuckle	31	2.8
Chinese privet	73	10.9
Black locust	74	14.5
Eastern redbud	27	16.9
American beech	27	17.4
Flowering dogwood	51	20.4
Black tupelo	41	23.5
Sassafras	40	23.8
Slippery elm	25	25.3
Sourwood	41	26.7

Damage Indicators of Forest Health

Signs of damage were recorded for all trees ≥1-inch d.b.h. Signs of damage were recorded based upon the location of the damage. Damage at the root level or tree bole can potentially be more significant in terms of tree health as compared to damages in branches or upper bole. The severity of the damage was also recorded. Up to three damages (see Glossary) were recorded per tree, with inspections starting at the roots and bole and progressing up the tree (U.S. Department of Agriculture 2005a).

The most common damages on trees were trunk bark inclusions (8.7 percent) and vines in crowns (7.9 percent) (table 14). Trunk bark inclusions are places where branches are not strongly attached to the tree. A weak union occurs when two or more branches grow so closely together that bark grows between the branches and inside the union. This ingrown, or included, bark does not have the structural strength of wood and the union can become very weak. The inside bark may also act as a wedge and force the branch union to split apart. The land use with the greatest proportion of trees with trunk bark inclusions was commercial/industrial (table 14). Species with the highest percent of its population with trunk bark inclusions were sycamore and callery pear (table 15). Poor pruning practices can result in the formation of included trunk bark. Vines in the crown affect tree growth where their leaves displace the leaves of the tree. The tree with fewer leaves and less ability to photosynthesize will begin to decline as the vines become more dominant. Vines that tend to be troublesome in Tennessee include poison ivy, kudzu, wild grape, oriental bittersweet, and honeysuckle.

Dead and dying crown was the third most common damage (3.2 percent) with mimosa, sweetgum, and post oak having the highest percent of its population exhibiting this damage (table 15). A dead or dying top can be a sign of tree stress caused by disease or environmental factors such as soil compaction, or insufficient moisture or light. Cankers or signs of

Table 14—Percent of trees with various types of damage by land use, Tennessee, 2005–09

Damage type	Agriculture	Commercial/ industrial	Forest	Other urban	Residential	Transportation	Total
				percent			
Trunk/bark inclusion	0.8	22.6	5.3	10.3	15.4	15.1	8.7
Vines in crown	18.5	2.6	6.7	4.7	5.1	13.5	7.9
Dead/dying crown	4.4	2.6	3.1	1.0	2.8	4.8	3.2
Canker/decay	6.2	3.2	1.8	7.5	3.4	3.1	2.9
Wound/crack	0.3	1.3	1.7	7.1	2.7	1.5	2.1
Defoliation	0.5	0.0	2.4	0.0	0.3	1.4	1.6
Dead top	0.8	0.0	1.9	0.0	3.0	0.3	1.6
Chlorotic/necrotic foliage	0.5	0.0	0.2	0.0	2.3	1.2	0.6
Root/stem girdling	0.0	0.0	0.1	2.6	0.5	0.0	0.3
Borers/bark beetles	0.0	0.0	0.3	0.0	0.5	0.1	0.3

Table 15—Species with greatest proportion of their population classified as having the specific damage class (e.g., 5.5 percent of silver maples had borers/bark beetles), Tennessee, 2005–09

Damage class and species	Damage class	Damage class and species	Damage class
	percent		*percent*
Borers/bark beetles		Defoliation	
Silver maple	5.5	Green ash	14.4
Hackberry	3.0	Mockernut hickory	12.0
Loblolly pine	1.6	Black cherry	11.3
Chestnut oak	0.7	Pecan	9.5
(all other species)	0.0	Winged elm	9.4
Canker/decay		Root/stem girdling	
Mimosa	27.6	Callery pear	23.3
Sourwood	13.1	Water oak	12.1
Pecan	10.5	Osage orange	4.9
Shagbark hickory	8.7	White ash	3.1
Flowering dogwood	8.4	Sugarberry	1.1
Chlorotic/necrotic foliage		Trunk/bark inclusion	
American elm	16.1	Sycamore	60.8
Post oak	5.0	Callery pear	60.8
Flowering dogwood	3.7	Other species	38.9
Sycamore	3.2	Eastern white pine	31.7
Black cherry	1.8	Water oak	29.4
Dead/dying crown		Vines in crown	
Mimosa	23.9	Cherrybark oak	25.2
Sweetgum	17.5	Black cherry	24.7
Post oak	16.6	Winged elm	21.4
Black walnut	14.0	Eastern redcedar	20.6
Eastern redbud	11.8	American beech	20.4
Dead top		Wound/crack	
Shagbark hickory	28.3	Mimosa	23.9
Eastern redbud	14.1	Callery pear	23.3
Sweetgum	10.7	Osage orange	17.0
Water oak	6.7	Post oak	10.5
Black cherry	6.5	Sourwood	10.1

Note: Only species with minimum sample size of 10 trees are included in this analysis to minimize effect of small sample size on percentage estimates. All species values are given in appendices E and F.

decay were the fourth most common damage and was found in 2.9 percent of the trees. Decay is a serious concern in urban areas since the presence of wood decay increases the potential for tree failure. Mimosa, sourwood, and pecan had the highest proportion of population with cankers and signs of decay (table 15). The diameter distribution of trees with damage tended to have an inverse-J shape, but to varying degrees (fig. 24). Damages that tended to occur more on larger trees were wounds/cracks,

cankers/decay, borers/bark beetles, and root/stem girdling. Damage that was most frequent on smaller trees was defoliation.

In addition to the tree damages in table 14, 0.7 percent of the trees were noted as having conflicts with overhead wires, 0.7 percent with topping and pruning damage, 0.3 percent with improper planting, and 0.1 percent sidewalk/root conflicts (table 16). Residential trees had the highest percent of its population with these maintenance and site issues.

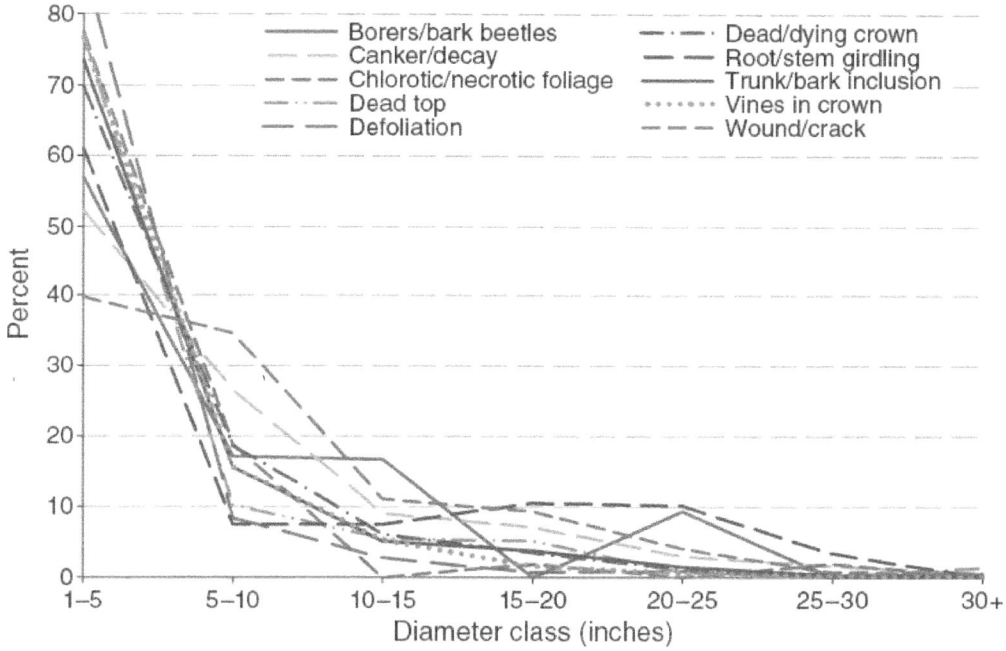

Figure 24—Diameter distribution of trees with various damage types, Tennessee, 2005–09.

Table 16—Percent of trees with site or maintenance issue by land use, Tennessee, 2005–09

Site or maintenance issue	Agriculture	Commercial/ industrial	Forest	Other urban	Residential	Transportation	Total
				percent			
Overhead wires	0.0	0.0	0.1	0.6	3.4	1.1	0.7
Topping/pruning	0.0	0.0	0.0	0.0	3.2	1.6	0.7
Improper planting	0.0	0.0	0.0	0.0	2.3	0.0	0.3
Sidewalk-root conflict	0.0	0.0	0.0	0.2	0.3	0.0	0.1
Excess mulch	0.0	0.0	0.0	0.0	0.2	0.0	0.0

Ecosystem Services and Values

Carbon Storage by Urban Trees

Climate change is an issue of global concern. Urban trees can help mitigate climate change by sequestering atmospheric carbon (from carbon dioxide) in plant tissue and by reducing energy use in buildings, consequently reducing carbon dioxide emissions from fossil-fuel based power plants (Abdollahi and others 2000).

Trees can reduce the amount of carbon in the atmosphere by providing a net increase in new growth (carbon) every year (i.e., growth > decomposition). The amount of carbon annually sequestered is typically greatest in large healthy trees. Trees and forests are considered a significant sink of carbon within terrestrial ecosystems. The process by which a tree removes carbon from the atmosphere is called carbon sequestration. The amount or weight of carbon currently accumulated by a tree is considered carbon storage. To estimate the monetary value associated with urban tree carbon storage and sequestration, carbon values were multiplied by $20.7 per ton of carbon based on the estimated marginal social costs of carbon dioxide emissions for 2000-10 (Fankhauser 1994).

Carbon storage by Tennessee's urban forest is estimated at 16.9 million tons (62.0 million tons of CO_2) ($350 million). The species that are estimated to sequester the most carbon annually are chestnut oak (7.2 percent of the total annual sequestration), hackberry (5.7 percent), and yellow-poplar (4.3 percent) (fig. 25). Sequestration estimates are based on estimates of growth, which are partially dependent upon tree condition. Annual carbon sequestration by urban trees is valued at $18.4 million per year (table 17).

Heating and Cooling Effects of Urban Trees

Trees affect energy consumption of buildings by shading buildings, providing evaporative cooling, and by blocking winter winds. Trees tend to reduce energy use in the summer and either increase or decrease the building energy use in the winter depending upon their location around the building. Tree effects on building energy use were based on field measurements of tree distance and direction to residential buildings.

In Tennessee, interactions between trees and buildings are projected to save homeowners $66 million annually based on 2007 energy costs. Costs in winter are estimated to increase by about $29 million per year, while energy savings in the summer are

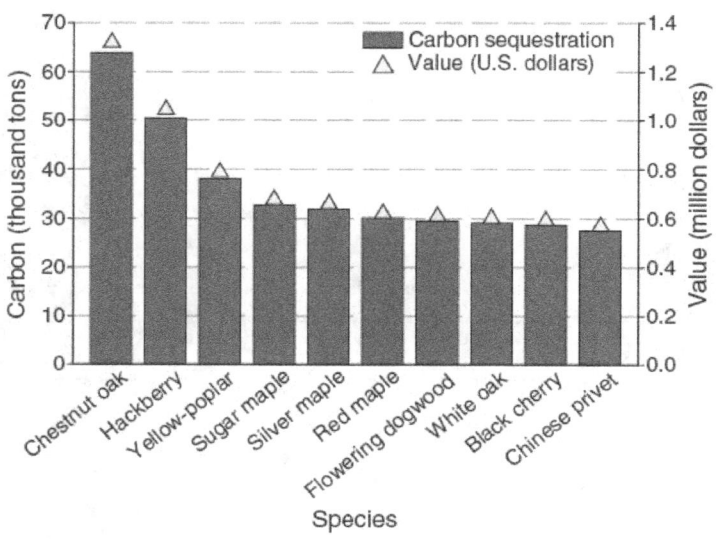

Figure 25—Annual carbon sequestration by top 10 species in terms of estimated annual gross carbon sequestration, Tennessee, 2005–09.

Table 17—Carbon storage and annual sequestration by land use, Tennessee, 2005–09

Land use	Carbon storage		Sequestration	
	tons	*dollars*	*tons per year*	*dollars per year*
Forest	7,407,000	153,252,000	396,000	8,184,000
Residential	4,135,000	85,553,000	207,000	4,277,000
Transportation	2,549,000	52,744,000	145,000	3,006,000
Other urban	1,698,000	35,123,000	84,000	1,747,000
Agriculture	757,000	15,656,000	39,000	810,000
Commercial/industrial	392,000	8,119,000	19,000	386,000
Total urban	16,938,000	350,447,000	890,000	18,411,000

estimated at $95 million per year. Because of reduced building energy use, power plants will burn less fossil fuel and, therefore, release less carbon dioxide. Changes in energy use will lead to reduced emission of carbon of about 180,000 tons per year (660,000 tons of carbon dioxide per year) in Tennessee with an estimated value of $3.7 million per year.

Air Pollution Removal by Urban Trees

Poor air quality is a common problem in urban areas and leads to human health problems, ecosystem damage, and reduced visibility. The urban forest can improve air quality by reducing ambient air temperatures, removing pollutants directly from the air, and reducing the energy use in buildings. However, trees emit volatile organic compounds (VOCs) that can contribute to ground level ozone formation. Yet, integrated studies have revealed that increasing tree cover can ultimately reduce ozone formation (Nowak 2005).

Pollution removal by Tennessee's urban forest is estimated with the use of hourly pollution data from all the monitors in the State and weather data (Nashville) from the year 2000. Based on these inputs, the urban forests in Tennessee are estimated to remove about 27,100 tons of pollution per year, with an associated annual value of about $203.9 million. Pollutant removal rate was greatest for ozone (O_3) followed by particulate matter < 10 microns (PM_{10}), sulfur dioxide (SO_2), nitrogen dioxide (NO_2), and carbon monoxide (CO) (fig. 26).

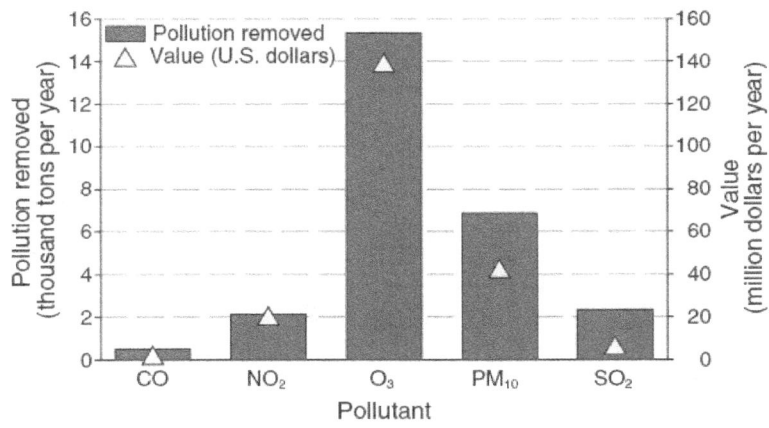

Figure 26—Annual pollution removal and value from urban trees, Tennessee, 2005–09. CO = carbon monoxide, NO_2 = nitrogen dioxide, O_3 = ozone, PM_{10} = coarse particulate matter, SO_2 = sulfur dioxide.

Value of Tennessee's Urban Forest

Urban forests have a structural value based on the tree resource itself (e.g., the cost of having to replace a tree with a similar tree), and annually produce functional values based on the functions the tree performs. These estimates annual values can be either positive (e.g., air pollution removal, reduced building energy use) or negative (e.g., volatile organic compound emissions, increased building energy use) depending upon species and tree location. In North America, the most widely used method for estimating the compensatory or structural value of trees was developed by the Council of Tree and Landscape Appraisers (CTLA) (Council of Tree and Landscape Appraisers 2000). Compensatory values represent compensation to owners for the loss of an individual tree. Compensatory values can be used for estimating compensation for tree losses, justifying and managing resources, and/or setting policies related to the management of urban trees. CTLA compensatory value calculations are based on tree and site characteristics, specifically: tree trunk area (cross-sectional area at 4.5 feet above the ground), species, condition, and location (see Nowak and others 2008 for detailed methods).

The estimated structural value of Tennessee's urban forest is about $79.5 billion. Other estimated functional values of the urban forest include carbon storage ($350.4 million), annual carbon sequestration ($18.4 million per year), annual pollution removal ($203.9 million per year) and annual building energy reduction ($66.0 million per year) (table 18). These values tend to increase with increased size and number of healthy trees.

Table 18—Value of urban forest–monetary value of urban forest structure and annual functions, Tennessee, 2005–09

Benefit	Value
	U.S. dollars
Structural value	79.5 billion
Carbon storage	350.4 million
Carbon sequestration	18.4 million
Pollution removal	203.9 million
Energy reduction	66.0 million

Potential Risk to Pests

Based on the species distribution, the urban forest is at risk from various pests that could potentially impact the health and sustainability of the urban forest resource (fig. 27). Seven native or exotic pests and diseases were analyzed using the i-Tree Eco model. These pests and diseases were: southern pine beetle (*Dendroctonus frontalis*), hemlock woolly adelgid (*Adelges tsugae*), thousand cankers disease

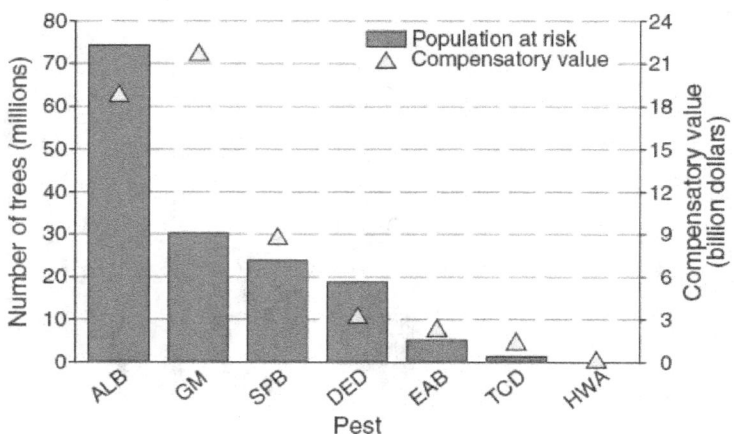

Figure 27—Estimated potential impact of pests on urban tree population, Tennessee. ALB = Asian longhorned beetle, GM = gypsy moth, SPB = southern pine beetle, DED = Dutch elm disease, EAB = emerald ash borer, TCD = thousand cankers disease, and HWA = hemlock woolly adelgid.

[(caused by the fungus *Geosmithia morbida* and vector walnut twig beetle (*Pityophthorous juglandis*)], Asian longhorned beetle (*Anoplophora glabripennis*), gypsy moth (*Lymantria dispar*), emerald ash borer (*Agrilus planipennis*), and Dutch elm disease (*Ophiostoma ulmi*).

The thousand cankers disease is a recently discovered insect-disease complex that kills black walnuts (fig. 28). Tennessee is the first State in the East where thousand cankers disease has been found. Trees often are killed within 3 years after initial symptoms are noticed. Tree mortality is the result of attack by the walnut twig beetle and subsequent canker development around beetle galleries caused by associated fungi (Cranshaw and Tisserat 2009). In urban Tennessee there are 1.2 million black walnuts (compensatory value of $1.3 billion) that could be lost to this disease. Outside of the urban boundary there are an estimated 28 million black walnut trees in Tennessee that are threatened by this insect-disease complex.

The southern pine beetle is one of pine's most destructive insect enemies in the Southern United States. Because populations build rapidly to outbreak proportions and large numbers of trees are killed, this insect is of significant concern in southern pine forests (Thatcher and Barry 1982). About 24 million urban pine trees ($8.7 billion) could be affected by this beetle in Tennessee. Since 1999, a considerable area of forest land in Tennessee has been impacted by

the southern pine beetle and is often cited as one of the main factors contributing to the decline of pine forest types statewide (Oswalt and others 2009).

The hemlock woolly adelgid is a small, aphid-like insect native to Asia that threatens eastern and Carolina hemlock populations in the Eastern United States. First reported in the Eastern United States in 1951, this pest has now become established in portions of 16 States from Maine to Georgia, where infestations cover about one-half of the range of hemlock. The impact of this pest (tree mortality and decline) has been most severe in some areas of Virginia, New Jersey, Pennsylvania, and Connecticut (U.S. Department of Agriculture 2005b). There are about 66,000 hemlock trees ($43.9 million) that could be attacked by this pest in urban Tennessee. Outside of the urban boundary, however, there are an estimated 91 million hemlock trees that are vulnerable.

The Asian longhorned beetle is an insect that bores into and kills a wide range of hardwood species. This beetle was discovered in 1996 in Brooklyn, New York and has subsequently spread to Long Island, Queens, and Manhattan. In 1998, the beetle was discovered in the suburbs of Chicago, Illinois. Beetles have also been found in Jersey City, New York (2002), Toronto/Vaughan, Ontario (2003) and Middlesex/Union Counties, New Jersey (2004). In 2007, the beetle was found on Staten and Prall's Island, New York. Most recently, beetles were detected in

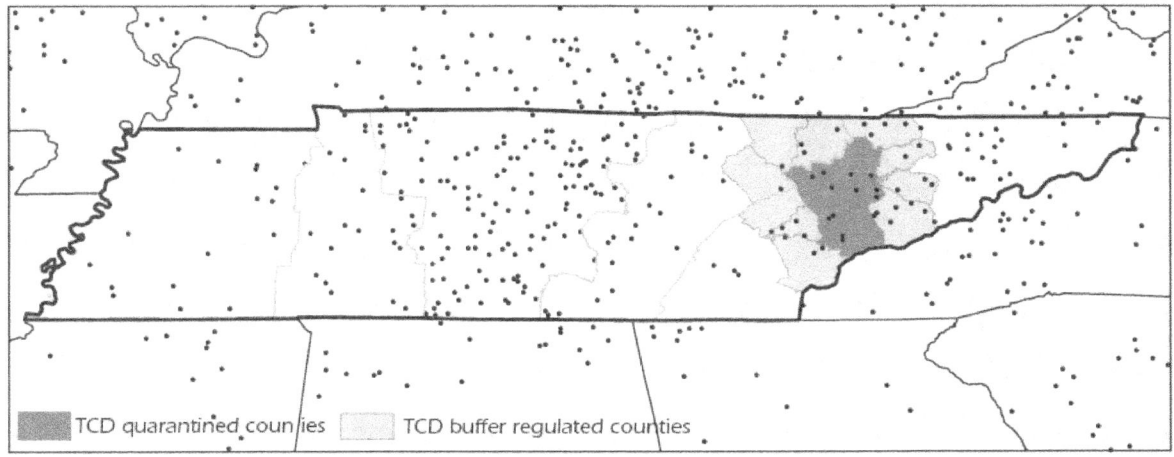

TCD quarantined counties   TCD buffer regulated counties

FIA plot locations are approximate

Figure 28—Approximate location of sampled black walnut and recent thousand cankers disease (TCD) quarantined counties and buffer regulated counties in Tennessee (county designations according to Tennessee Department of Agriculture Division of Forestry). Note: Additonal counties may have been added since development of this publication.

Worcester, Massachusetts (2008) (U.S. Department of Agriculture 2002, U.S. Department of Agriculture Animal and Plant Health Inspection Service 2010, Natural Resources Canada 2010). In urban Tennessee, this beetle represents a potential loss of $18.7 billion in structural value (26.4 percent of live tree population).

The gypsy moth is a defoliator that feeds on many species causing widespread defoliation and tree death if outbreak conditions last several years (Liebhold 2003, U.S. Department of Agriculture 2005). This pest could potentially result in damage to or a loss of $20.6 billion in structural value of urban Tennessee's trees (10.8 percent of live tree population). If one assumes that only about 20 percent of the population will be killed in a large gypsy moth outbreak, the risk to this pest drops to $4.3 billion (2.2 percent of the population).

Since being discovered in Detroit, Michigan in 2002, the emerald ash borer has killed millions of ash trees in Illinois, Indiana, Kentucky, Maryland, Michigan, Minnesota, Missouri, New York, Ohio, Ontario, Pennsylvania, Quebec, Tennessee, Virginia, West Virginia, and Wisconsin (U.S. Department of Agriculture and others 2010). Emerald ash borer has the potential to affect 1.8 percent of urban Tennessee's live tree population ($2.2 billion in structural value) (fig. 29).

American elm, one of the most important street trees in the 20th century, has been devastated by the Dutch elm disease. Since first reported in the 1930s, it has killed > 50 percent of the native elm population in the United States (Stack and others 1996). Although some elm species have shown varying degrees of resistance, urban Tennessee possibly could lose 6.7 percent of its live trees to this disease ($3.1 billion in structural value).

Discussion

Urban trees in Tennessee are mostly found within forest stands, transportation corridors and residential land uses. These land uses account for about 64 percent of the urban area and 85 percent of the urban tree population. An estimated 15 percent of the urban forest area is comprised of forests similar in nature to those forests outside of the urban boundary (i.e., classified as forest land use) and have historically been captured in the forest resource assessments conducted by the FIA program in the past. With the advent of this urban forest inventory, we now have the capability of further describing the forests resources in Tennessee with greater detail by including those valuable forests within residential communities, along transportation routes, surrounding local commercial operations, along with other areas not included in traditional forest inventories.

FIA plot locations are approximate

Figure 29—Approximate location of sampled ash species and recent emerald ash borer (EAB) quarantined counties in Tennessee (county designations according to Tennessee Department of Agriculture Division of Forestry). Note: Additonal counties may have been added since development of this publication.

Statewide, forests cover about 14 million acres (Oswalt and others 2009). When the 1.3 million acres of urban forests that are outside of the traditional FIA analyses are included, forests and urban forests together account for about 57 percent of the total land base in Tennessee. Urban forests are an important resource within the State. Moreover, trees and forests in urban areas that are not currently sampled by the FIA program, but were included in this study, will become increasingly important as the extent of urban land is predicted to more than double in the State of Tennessee by 2050 (Nowak and Walton 2005).

There are an estimated 284 million trees distributed across the 1.6 million acres of urban forests in the State. Over one-half (about 56 percent) of urban trees were located in areas with a forested land use. Tree density on forest land within the urban boundary (685 trees per acre) is higher than the average tree density statewide of 569 trees per acre. The lowest average tree density and least number of trees was observed on urban forests within commercial/industrial land uses.

The urban forests of Tennessee are fairly diverse, with only one species (Chinese privet) comprising ≥10 percent of the existing population. The shrubby Chinese privet is not a species that immediately comes to mind when one pictures the typical trees found in Tennessee's urban areas. However, it is important and instructive to note the abundance of this nonnative, originally ornamental species, and amur honeysuckle, makeup 15 percent of the trees found by this study. Continued evaluation and monitoring will indicate whether these species remain, expand their distributions, or if new species are introduced into these urban forests.

Many of the larger trees found in urban Tennessee, such as yellow-poplar, chestnut oak, white oak (highest basal area), hackberry, and flowering dogwood (most leaf area) and other common species such as callery pear, silver maple, and eastern white pine (most frequently found in maintained areas), are more reflective of the urban forests Tennesseans are accustomed to seeing around them every day.

The urban forests sampled in Tennessee had fewer species collected within the urban boundary than have been observed statewide. Within the urban boundary 99 different species were identified, whereas 119 different species were identified across

forests statewide (one species was only found within the urban boundary). This difference is expected as a wider variety of habitats and increased number of plots, and therefore tree species, can be found statewide than is found within Tennessee's urban areas. However, urban areas often introduce new species to an area. Thus, distinct differences appear when comparing the composition of trees within urban forests to that of forests statewide. For example, the most common tree >5 inches d.b.h. found within urban forests is eastern redcedar, followed by hackberry, Virginia pine, yellow-poplar, and chestnut oak. However, the most common tree >5 inches d.b.h. in forests statewide are white oak, red maple, yellow-poplar, chestnut oak, and loblolly pine. The common species >5 inches d.b.h. in urban forests, for the most part, represent younger forests whereas those species common statewide represent more mature forests. Upon comparing common trees within individual land use classes with common species statewide further divergence exists between the urban and nonurban forests. Virginia pine is the most common species on transportation and residential land uses, Chinese privet on forested land use within the urban boundary and other land use, hackberry is the most common on agricultural land uses, and hawthorn on commercial land use urban forests. Red maple is the most commonly found tree across the State, representing almost 10 percent of all trees in Tennessee.

The urban forests of Tennessee provide significant social and environmental benefits to the people of Tennessee. The resource itself is worth billions of dollars. The 284.1 million urban trees in Tennessee have an estimated structural value of $79 billion, provide an annual energy saving to residents of $66 million, annually remove $204 million worth of pollution from the air, and store 16.9 million tons of carbon valued at $350 million. Many other environmental and social benefits are yet to be quantified. Sustaining forest health and longevity is critical to sustaining these benefits through time.

With few exceptions that need to be monitored, the trees in Tennessee's urban forests are relatively healthy. Overall there were few indicators of stress, loss of vigor, and the resultant susceptibility to the pest and diseases such as crown dieback, decreases in crown density, and other damages (Anderson and others 1979). However, dead and dying trees can be

removed relatively quickly in urban areas, leaving behind the appearance of a more healthy forest that would be assessed by field crews. Long-term monitoring of these plots will provide better data on long-term health, condition, and change in the urban forest. The relatively higher rates of crown dieback and frequency of standing dead individuals for black walnut needs to be investigated further to determine whether these signs of lost vigor are related to infection by thousand cankers disease. Movement of hemlock woolly adelgids into urban areas near infected forests should also be monitored closely. Fortunately, black walnuts and hemlocks do not makeup a large percentage (<1 percent each) of the trees in these urban forests.

Conclusion

With the growth of urban areas and high concentration of human populations in urban areas, data on urban forests are becoming more essential, particularly as urban trees can have significant impacts on numerous local to global environmental regulations (e.g., Clean Air Act, Clean Water Act). Having long-term data on this important resource will allow urban trees and forests to be assessed for how their forest composition and associated ecosystem values are changing. In addition, monitoring can provide essential data in relation to the potential use of urban forests in regulations set to protect human health and well-being. Not only does an urban forest monitoring program provide essential data for management and integration with local to international policies, the long-term data provide essential information for sustaining urban forest canopy cover and health.

Management of any natural resource requires knowledge of type, size, and quantity of the resource. Inventories and assessments to monitor composition, size, and health provide information about the current status of urban forests, and, if compiled periodically, information about how the forest changes over time. The current study is the first statewide inventory and FHM effort to quantify the urban forests within the State of Tennessee. If the pilot protocol were to be implemented into a regular inventory and assessment, resource managers would

be able to monitor how urban forests change over time due to urbanization pressures, management techniques, and the influence of stresses, such as invasive pests or extreme weather events. In addition, information could be compiled on which species perform the best under differing urban conditions and how long various species live on average in urban areas.

Statewide estimates of urban forest and tree resources only exist for a few States in addition to Tennessee (Indiana and Wisconsin) (Nowak and others 2007, Cumming and others 2007), but no State has a long-term urban forest monitoring program. The State urban forest data collected has enabled an estimation of urban forest statistics including biomass, carbon storage, energy savings, air pollution removal, and structural value. Data collected here can be used as a baseline from which changes and trends can be evaluated if the plots are remeasured. Using i-Tree Eco, economic impacts associated with selected potential pest problems were determined. While species composition data alone could be used to describe the potential susceptibility of the Tennessee urban forest to various pests, use of i-Tree Eco enabled an economic impact assessment that included structural or compensatory values.

To sustain the health, environmental, and social benefits received from urban forests, specific urban forest management plans and goals need to be developed. These plans also need to be dynamic due to the continuous forces of change that alter urban forest environments. Long-term urban forest monitoring data will provide the information necessary to make these specific, goal-oriented management plans. In addition, the monitoring data will allow for assessments of the success of the plans and continual updating of plans to ensure forest sustainability. Long-term monitoring data will also reveal what factors (e.g., insects, diseases, decay, etc.) most threaten urban forest sustainability so corrective management actions can be taken. Data from urban forest monitoring programs should be incorporated within State and local urban forest planning and management regimes to allow local constituents to develop canopy goals and/or tree planting goals to sustain or enhance urban forest canopy across the State.

Acknowledgments

This report highlights the findings from the first statewide urban FHM pilot study conducted in the State of Tennessee. In addition to the authors, personnel involved in compiling this report were: Bill Smith and Daniel Crane, USDA Forest Service, and the Information Management staff, USDA Forest Service, Morgantown, West Virginia field office.

We would like to thank the following groups and people for their support and funding of this project: Tennessee Division of Forestry: John Ferris, Brent Lecher, Michael Holder, Jamie Meyer, Douglas Godbee, Shawn Hendrickson, John Mullins, Jason O'Shell, Steven Hacker, Ellen Gray, Danny Osborne, Brian Rucker, Travis Trainer, Stephen Peairs, and Bruce Webster. USDA Forest Service: Lyndell Davidson, Vince Few, Sarah Combs, Anita Rose, Kelly Peterson. FIA Urban Task Team: Anita Rose, Dale Gormanson, Mark Majewsky, David Alerich, Randall Morin, James Westfall, Barb O'Connell, Bill Dunning, Chuck Liff, Angie Rowe, Dave Latelle, Bruce Webster, Rachel Riemann, Vince Few, and John Mullins.

Literature Cited

Abdollahi, K.K.; Ning, Z.H.; Appeaning A., eds. 2000. Global climate change and the urban forest. Baton Rouge, LA: Franklin Press: Gulf Coast Regional Climate Change Council. [Pages unknown].

Anderson, R.L.; Anderson, G.W. (revised by Schipper, A.L.). 1979. Hypoxylon canker of aspen. Forest insect and disease leaflet 6. http://www.na.fs.fed.us/spfo/pubs/fidls/hypoxylon/hypoxylon.htm. [Date accessed unknown].

Bratkovich, S.M. 2001. Utilizing municipal trees: ideas from across the country. Tech. Pub. NA–TP–06–01. St. Paul, MN: U.S. Department of Agriculture Forest Service, Northeastern Area State and Private Forestry. [Not paged]. http://www.na.fs.fed.us/Spfo/pubs/misc/utilizingmunitrees/index.htm#TOC. [Date accessed unknown].

Conkling, B.L.; Byers, G.E., eds. 1992. Forest health monitoring field methods guide. Las Vegas, NV: U.S. Environmental Protection Agency; Internal report. [Pages unknown].

Council of Tree and Landscape Appraisers. 2000. Guide for plant appraisal. 9th ed. Champaign, IL: International Society of Arboriculture. 143 p.

Cranshaw, W.; Tisserat, N. 2009. Walnut twig beetle and thousand cankers disease of black walnut. Pest Alert. Ft. Collins, CO: Colorado State University. [Not paged]. http://www.ext.colostate.edu/pubs/insect/0812_alert.pdf. [Date accessed unknown].

Cumming, A.B.; Galvin, M.F.; Rabaglia, R.J. [and others]. 2001. Forest health monitoring protocol applied to roadside trees in Maryland. Journal of Arboriculture. 27(3): 126–138.

Cumming, A.B.; Nowak, D.J.; Twardus, D.B. [and others]. 2007. Urban forests of Wisconsin: pilot monitoring project 2002. NA–FR–05–07. Newtown Square, PA: U.S. Department of Agriculture Forest Service, Northeastern Area State and Private Forestry Report. 33 p.

Fankhauser, S. 1994. The social costs of greenhouse gas emissions: an expected value approach. The Energy Journal. 15(2): 157–184.

Liebhold, A. 2003. Gypsy moth in North America. Morgantown, WV: U.S. Department of Agriculture Forest Service, Northeastern Research Station. www.fs.fed.us/ne/morgantown/4557/gmoth. [Date accessed unknown].

Little, E.L., Jr. 1979. Checklist of United States trees (native and naturalized). Agric. Handb. 541. Washington, DC: U.S. Department of Agriculture. 375 p.

Miles, P.D. 2011. Forest inventory EVALIDator web-application version 4.01 beta. St. Paul, MN: U.S. Department of Agriculture Forest Service, Northern Research Station. http://fiatools.fs.fed.us/Evalidator4/tmattribute.jsp. [Date accessed: March 17].

Natural Resources Canada. 2010. Sustainability indicators—asian longhorned beetle. http://canadaforests.nrcan.gc.ca/indicator/asianlonghornedbeetle. [Date accessed unknown].

Nowak, D.J. 2005. The effects of urban trees on air quality. Syracuse, NY: U.S. Department of Agriculture Forest Service, Northern Research Station. www.fs.fed.us/ne/syracuse/TREE%20Air%20Qual.pdf. [Date accessed unknown].

Nowak, D.J.; Crane, D.E.; Stevens, J.C. [and others]. 2008. A ground-based method of assessing urban forest structure and ecosystem services. Arboriculture and Urban Forestry. 34(6): 347–358.

Nowak, D.J.; Cumming, A.B.; Twardus, D.B. [and others]. 2007. Monitoring urban forests in Indiana: pilot study 2002, part 2: statewide estimates using the UFORE model. NA–FR–01–07. Newtown Square, PA: U.S. Department of Agriculture Forest Service, Northeastern Area, State and Private Forestry. 13 p.

Nowak, D.J.; Dwyer, J.F. 2007. Understanding the benefits and costs of urban forest ecosystems. In: Kuser, J.E., ed. Urban and community forestry in the northeast, 2d ed. New York: Springer: 25–46.

Nowak, D.J.; Walton, J.T. 2005. Projected urban growth (2000-2050) and its estimated impact on US forest resource. Journal of Forestry. 103(8): 383–389.

Nowak, D.J.; Walton, J.T.; Dwyer, J.F. [and others]. 2005. The increasing influence of urban environments on US forest management. Journal of Forestry. 103(8): 377–382.

Oswalt, C.M.; Oswalt, S.N.; Johnson, T.G. [and others]. 2009. Tennessee's forests, 2004. Resour. Bull. SRS–144. Asheville, NC: U.S. Department of Agriculture Forest Service, Southern Research Station. 96 p.

Stack, R.W.; McBride, D.K.; Lamey, H.A. 1996. Dutch elm disease. PP–324. Revised. Fargo, ND: North Dakota State University, Cooperative Extension Service. http://www.ext.nodak.edu/extpubs/plantsci/trees/pp324w.htm. [Date accessed unknown].

Steinman, J. 1998. Tracking the health of trees over time on forest health monitoring plots. In: Hansen, M.; Burk, T., eds. Integrating tools for natural resources inventories in the 21st century. Gen. Tech. Rep. NC–212. St. Paul, MN: U.S. Department of Agriculture Forest Service, North Central Forest Experiment Station: 334–339.

Thatcher, R.C.; Barry, P.J. 1982. Southern pine beetle. Forest Insect and Disease Leaflet 49. Washington, DC: U.S. Department of Agriculture Forest Service. 7 p.

U.S. Department of Agriculture Animal and Plant Health Inspection Service. 2010. Plant health—Asian longhorned beetle. http://www.aphis.usda.gov/plant_health/plant_pest_info/asian_lhb/index.shtml. [Date accessed unknown].

U.S. Department of Agriculture Forest Service [and others]. 2010. Emerald ash borer. http://www.emeraldashborer.info/. [Date accessed unknown].

U.S. Department of Agriculture Forest Service. 2002. Asian longhorned beetle (*Anoplophora glabripennis*): a new introduction. Pest Alert NA–PR–01–99GEN. Newtown Square, PA: U.S. Department of Agriculture Forest Service, Northeastern Area, State and Private Forestry. [Not paged]. www.na.fs.fed.us/spfo/pubs/pest_al/alb/index.htm. [Date accessed unknown].

U.S. Department of Agriculture Forest Service. 2005. Gypsy moth digest. Newtown Square, PA: U.S. Department of Agriculture Forest Service, Northeastern Area State and Private Forestry. http://www.na.fs.fed.us/fhp/gm/. [Date accessed unknown].

U.S. Department of Agriculture Forest Service. 2005a. Forest inventory and analysis national core field guide. Volume I: field data collection procedures for phase 2 plots, version 3.0. http://www.fia.fs.fed.us/library/field-guides-methods-proc/docs/2006/core_ver_3-0_10_2005.pdf. [Date accessed: April 2009].

U.S. Department of Agriculture Forest Service. 2005b. Hemlock woolly adelgid. Pest Alert NA–PR–09–05. Newtown Square, PA: U.S. Department of Agriculture Forest Service, Northeastern Area, State and Private Forestry. [Not paged]. http://www.na.fs.fed.us/spfo/pubs/pest_al/hemlock/hwa_05.pdf. [Date accessed unknown].

U.S. Department of Agriculture Forest Service. 2006. Forest inventory and analysis national field manual. Urban inventory pilot supplement. Section 15: urban measurements and sampling. Knoxville, TN: U.S. Department of Agriculture Forest Service. 68 p.

U.S. Department of Agriculture Forest Service. 2007. Forest inventory and analysis national core field guide. Phase 3 field guide–crowns: measurements and sampling. Version 4.0. http://www.fia.fs.fed.us/library/field-guides-methods-proc/docs/2007/p3_4-0_sec12_10_2007.pdf. [Date accessed: April 2009].

U.S. Department of Agriculture Forest Service. 2010. Forest inventory and analysis national core field guide: field data collection procedures for phase 2 plots. Version 5.0. Volume 1. Arlington, VA: U.S. Department of Agriculture Forest Service, Forest Inventory and Analysis Program. 361 p. www.fia.fs.fed.us/library/field-guides-methods-proc/. [Date assessed unknown].

U.S. Department of Agriculture Forest Service. 2011. Thousand cankers disease. Pest Alert NA–PR–02–10. Newtown Square, PA: U.S. Department of Agriculture Forest Service, Northeastern Area, State and Private Forestry. [Not paged].

U.S. Department of Agriculture Natural Resources Conservation Service. 2011. The PLANTS database. Greensboro, NC: National Plant Data Team. http://plants.usda.gov. [Data accessed unknown].

U.S. Department of Commerce, Bureau of the Census. 2007. www.census.gov. [Date accessed unknown].

U.S. Department of Commerce, Bureau of the Census. 2011. Urban and rural classification. http://www.census.gov/geo/www/ua/urbanruralclass.html. [Date accessed: September].

U.S. Department of Commerce, Bureau of the Census. 2011a. http://2010.census.gov/2010census/data/. [Date accessed unknown].

U.S. Department of Commerce, Bureau of the Census. 2011b. State interim population projections by age and sex: 2004-2030: ranking of census 2000 and projected 2030 state population and change. http://www.census.gov/population/www/projections/projectionsagesex.html. [Date accessed unknown].

Glossary

Crown—The part of a tree or woody plant bearing live branches or foliage.

Crown density—The amount of crown stem, branches, twigs, shoots, buds, foliage, and reproductive structures that block light penetration through the projected crown outline. Measured as a percentage.

Crown dieback—Recent mortality of branches with fine twigs, which begins at the terminal portion of a branch and proceeds toward the trunk. Dieback is only considered when it occurs in the upper and outer portions of the tree. Dead branches in the lower live crown are not considered as part of crown dieback, unless there is continuous dieback from the upper and outer crown down to those branches.

Damage/causal agents—

Trunk (canker or decay)—Presence of decay fungi; hollow areas or weak, rotten wood.

Trunk (wound or crack)—Physical damage to the main stem or stems of a tree. Bark is visibly damaged or absent. This includes: lightening strikes, lawn mower and line trimmer damage. Wound or crack must be at least 25 percent of circumference or over a 3 foot vertical section.

Roots (stem girdling)—Roots that encircle the trunk of tree may cause bark and wood tissue compression. Roots stem girdling must be at least 25 percent of circumference of stem at base.

Trunk/branches (bark inclusion)—"V" branching pattern. Signs of bark inclusion are evident. Bark inclusion is bark enclosed between branches with narrow angles of attachment, forming a wedge between the branches.

Trunk (severe topping or poor pruning)—Tree has been reduced to a single "pole" due to severe overpruning and branch removal. Poor pruning techniques include leaving stubs outside the branch collar, cutting into the branch collar. Severe topping or poor pruning must be ≥ 30 percent of crown.

Trunk (excessive mulch)—Mulch piled around the tree trunk. Root flare is not visible at base of trunk. Mulch piled high around stem and mulch depth > 8 inches.

Branches (dead or dying crown)—Dead branches in crown. Dead or dying crown must be ≥ 30 percent of crown.

Leaves (chlorotic/necrotic)—Leaves are chlorotic, necrotic, wilted, abnormal size/shape or have been defoliated from branches. Foliage chlorotic/necrotic must be ≥ 30 percent of crown.

Branches (vines in crown)—Vines present in tree. Vines in crown must be ≥ 30 percent of crown volume.

Main stem (dead top)—Dead top, main stem dead or missing. Main stem dead top must be at least 30 percent of tree height.

Sidewalk (conflict with roots)—Damage to sidewalk directly caused by roots.

Overhead wires (conflict with tree crown)—Tree crown (branches or leaves) are within 5 feet of utility wires.

Improper planting (trees ≤ 10 inches d.b.h.)—Evidence that burlap, twine, or root ball wire was not removed prior to planting. Any of the following are visible at the soil surface: burlap, twine, or cage/wire.

Diameter at breast height (d.b.h.)—The diameter for tree stem, located at 4.5 feet above the ground (breast height) on the uphill side of a tree. The point of diameter measurement may vary on abnormally formed trees.

Foliage transparency—The amount of skylight visible through microholes in the live portion of the crown, i.e. where you see foliage, normal or damaged, or remnants of its recent presence. Recently defoliated branches are included in foliage transparency measurements. Macroholes are excluded unless they are the result of recent defoliation. Dieback and dead branches are always excluded from the estimate. Foliage transparency is different from crown density because it emphasizes foliage and ignores stems, branches, fruits, and holes in the crown.

Forest land—Land that is at least 10 percent stocked by forest trees of any size, or land formerly having such tree cover, and is not currently developed for a nonforest use. The minimum area for classification as forest land is 1 acre. Roadside, streamside, and shelter-belt strips of timber must have a crown width at least 120 feet wide to qualify as forest land. Unimproved roads and trails, streams and other bodies of water, or natural clearings in forested areas shall be classified as forest, if <120 feet in width or 1.0 acre in size. Forest land is divided into timberland, reserved forest land, and other forest land (such as woodland).

i-Tree Eco—An i-Tree model formerly known as the Urban Forest Effects (UFORE) model that uses field data in conjunction with air pollution and meteorological inputs to quantify urban forest structure (such as species composition, tree density, tree health, leaf area, and biomass), environmental services (such as air pollution removal, carbon storage and sequestration, effects of trees on energy use), and potential pest impacts.

Land use—The purpose of human activity on the land; it is usually, but not always, related to land cover. Land use categories used were:

• Forest

• Residential (including multifamily residential)

• Commercial/industrial

• Transportation (limited access roadway, railway or airport; rights-of-way: improved road, maintained canals; utility)

• Agriculture (cropland, pasture, orchards, Christmas tree plantations, or idle farmland)

• Other (unclassified, water, wetlands, institutional, cemetery, vacant, parks, golf courses, beaches, barren land, marshes, and other lands not described above)

Census water—Rivers and streams that are >200 feet wide and bodies of water > 4.5 acres in size.

Noncensus water—Rivers, streams and other bodies of water that do not meet the requirements for census water.

Nonsampled—Not sampled due to denied access, hazardous conditions, being outside the United States or other reasons.

Maintained—The maintained classification was applied to each tree in our sample. It designates the surrounding area in which the tree is located. Maintained areas are regularly impacted by mowing, mulching, or other types of landscape care. It does not imply that the tree is maintained.

Tree—A woody perennial plant, typically large, with a single well-defined stem carrying a more or less definite crown; sometimes defined as attaining a minimum diameter of 3 inches and a minimum height of 15 feet at maturity. For FIA, any plant on the tree list in the current field manual is measured as a tree.

Urban—Urban areas were classified based on the 2000 census and consisted of: all territory, population, and housing units located within either urbanized areas or urban clusters (U.S. Department of Commerce 2011). Urbanized area and urban cluster boundaries encompass densely settled territories, which generally consist of: (a) cluster of one or more block groups or census blocks with a population density of at least 1,000 people per square mile, (b) surrounding block groups and census blocks with a population density of 500 people per square mile, and (c) less densely settled blocks that form enclaves or indentations, or are used to connect discontinuous areas. Urbanized areas consist of densely settled territory that has ≥ 50,000 people; urban clusters consist of densely settled territory that has ≥ 2,500 people but < 50,000 people.

Urban forest—Term used for all trees within the urban boundary (both forest and nonforest lands).

Metric Equivalents

1 acre = 4,046.86 m² or 0.404686 ha
1 cubic foot = 0.028317 m³
1 inch = 2.54 cm or 0.0254 m
Breast height = 1.374 m above the ground
1 square foot = 929.03 cm² or 0.0929 m²
1 square foot per basal area = 0.229568 m²/ha
1 cubic foot per acre = 0.0699722 m²/ha
1 pound = 0.454 kg
1 ton = 0.907 MT

Appendix A—Methods

The U.S. Department of Agriculture (USDA) Forest Service's Forest Inventory and Analysis (FIA) program annually assesses the Nation's forest resource on a statewide basis. Detailed tree measurements are collected on forest plots defined by FIA as areas at least 1 acre in size, at least 120 feet wide, and at least 10 percent stocked. Forested plots must also have an understory that is undisturbed by another land use (U.S. Department of Agriculture 2010). In 2001, the USDA Forest Service, Forest Health and Monitoring (FHM) program initiated an assessment of urban forest conditions. This assessment delimited urban boundaries and then collected tree information from established plots within the urban boundaries. Urban areas were classified based on the 2000 census and consisted of: (all territory, population, and housing units located within either urbanized areas or urban clusters (U.S. Department of Commerce 2011). Urbanized area and urban cluster boundaries encompass densely settled territories, which generally consist of: (a) cluster of one or more block groups or census blocks with a population density of at least 1,000 people per square mile, (b) surrounding block groups and census blocks with a population density of 500 people per square mile, and (c) less densely settled blocks that form enclaves or indentations, or are used to connect discontinuous areas. Urbanized areas consist of densely settled territory that contains ≥50,000 people; urban clusters consist of densely settled territory that has ≥2,500 people but <50,000 people. Plots were measured regardless of whether the plot met the FIA definition of forested land.

FIA plots are measured on a panel system in which about one-fifth of all the plots within a State are measured in a given year. This pilot study began collecting the first panel of plots in 2005, with a new panel collected each year until the fifth and final panel was collected in 2009. A total of 265 plots landed within the urban boundary. Four plots were in water and six were denied access. These plots were not measured. Over the 5-year period, 255 permanent field plots were established and measured (table A.1).

On each plot, trees and saplings were measured. Variables measured on the trees and the plot included: species, diameter, height, height to live crown, crown dimensions, foliage transparency, tree damage, distance of tree to buildings, ground cover, impervious surface in plot, condition class, and ownership. Each plot consisted of four subplots with microplots contained within the subplot (fig. A.1). Data were collected on all trees ≥5 inches d.b.h. on four 1/24th acre subplots and on saplings between 1 and 5 inches diameter at breast height (d.b.h.) on four 1/300th acre microplots (Data collection methods are described in detail in U.S. Department of Agriculture 2005a, 2006).

Methods of the assessment of ecosystem services using the i-Tree model are detailed in Nowak and others (2008). Additional forest health data were collected on urban trees in Tennessee, including estimates of tree crown condition (U.S. Department of Agriculture 2007) and tree damage (U.S. Department of Agriculture 2006).

Table A.1—Urban plots by land use/plot status in Tennessee, 2005–09

Land use/plot status	Sampled	
	Plots	Live trees
	number	
Forest	40	1,137
Transportation	60	326
Residential	72	463
Other urban	28	179
Agriculture	30	128
Commercial/industrial	25	47
Census defined water	4	na
Denied access or problem plot	6	na
Total	265	2,280

na = not applicable.
Sample intensity, nonwater = 1 plot per 6,111 acres.

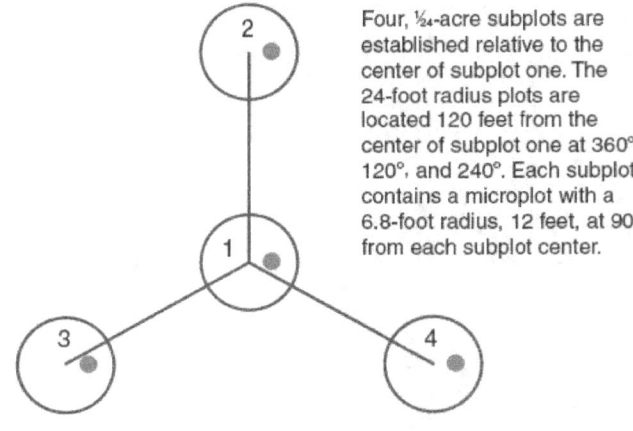

Four, ¼-acre subplots are established relative to the center of subplot one. The 24-foot radius plots are located 120 feet from the center of subplot one at 360°, 120°, and 240°. Each subplot contains a microplot with a 6.8-foot radius, 12 feet, at 90° from each subplot center.

Figure A.1—FIA plot configuration.

Appendix B—Statistics of Tree Species

Table B.1—Statistics of tree species by common and scientific name, Tennessee, 2005–09

Common name	Scientific name[a][b]	Trees	Percent of trees	Basal area			D.b.h. Average	D.b.h. Median
		- number -	percent	- - ft² - -	ft²/ac	percent	- - - - inches - - - -	
American basswood	Tilia americana	34,845	0.0	12,163	0.0	0.0	7.5	8.0
American beech	Fagus grandifolia	8,665,226	3.0	489,762	0.3	0.8	2.1	1.4
American elm	Ulmus americana	5,154,063	1.8	907,476	0.6	1.4	3.7	1.2
American holly	Ilex opaca	62,660	0.0	30,929	0.0	0.0	9.0	8.0
Amur honeysuckle	Lonicera maackii	12,965,648	4.6	495,096	0.3	0.8	2.0	1.2
Baldcypress	Taxodium distichum	337,903	0.1	478,840	0.3	0.7	14.5	13.2
Bitternut hickory	Carya cordiformis	860,179	0.3	465,858	0.3	0.7	7.8	3.0
Black birch	Betula lenta	34,845	0.0	27,367	0.0	0.0	11.5	12.0
Black cherry	Prunus serotina	7,808,122	2.7	1,549,208	1.0	2.4	4.5	4.4
Black locust	Robinia pseudoacacia	7,906,797	2.8	1,117,382	0.7	1.7	3.5	1.0
Black oak	Quercus velutina	1,165,417	0.4	1,085,815	0.7	1.7	11.7	9.0
Black tupelo	Nyssa sylvatica	8,746,938	3.1	1,071,382	0.7	1.6	3.4	2.1
Black walnut	Juglans nigra	1,247,642	0.4	974,994	0.6	1.5	10.8	9.1
Black willow	Salix nigra	324,164	0.1	178,055	0.1	0.3	8.8	7.1
Blackjack oak	Quercus marilandica	139,379	0.0	47,322	0.0	0.1	7.3	6.0
Blue ash	Fraxinus quadrangulata	104,535	0.0	49,790	0.0	0.1	8.8	8.3
Boxelder	Acer negundo	3,918,957	1.4	1,321,887	0.8	2.0	5.5	2.1
Bur oak	Quercus macrocarpa	31,330	0.0	33,492	0.0	0.1	13.5	14.0
Butternut	Juglans cinerea	134,230	0.0	125,172	0.1	0.2	12.5	11.3
Callery pear	Pyrus calleryana	2,445,968	0.9	328,777	0.2	0.5	4.0	4.7
Carolina hemlock	Tsuga caroliniana	31,330	0.0	10,936	0.0	0.0	7.5	8.0
Cherry	Prunus spp.	121,094	0.0	59,632	0.0	0.1	8.8	9.3
Cherrybark oak	Quercus pagoda	414,522	0.1	910,699	0.6	1.4	18.4	21.2
Chestnut oak	Quercus prinus	5,099,711	1.8	3,982,526	2.6	6.1	9.3	8.0
Chinese chestnut	Castanea mollissima	97,505	0.0	49,912	0.0	0.1	9.1	8.4
Chinese privet	Ligustrum sinense	29,676,844	10.4	1,109,929	0.7	1.7	1.9	1.3
Chinkapin oak	Quercus muehlenbergii	1,041,915	0.4	544,039	0.3	0.8	7.6	6.1
Cockspur hawthorn	Crataegus crus-galli	1,432,599	0.5	67,445	0.0	0.1	2.0	1.2
Common cherry laurel	Prunus laurocerasus	889,452	0.3	88,610	0.1	0.1	2.5	1.8
Common persimmon	Diospyros virginiana	2,239,172	0.8	212,939	0.1	0.3	3.1	2.2
Common plum	Prunus domestica	477,533	0.2	16,500	0.0	0.0	1.8	1.9
Crabapple	Malus spp.	93,989	0.0	28,366	0.0	0.0	6.8	6.3
Dahoon holly	Ilex cassine	62,660	0.0	12,645	0.0	0.0	5.5	4.0
Eastern cottonwood	Populus deltoides	277,026	0.1	476,256	0.3	0.7	15.5	12.1
Eastern hemlock	Tsuga canadensis	34,845	0.0	9,312	0.0	0.0	6.5	7.0
Eastern hophornbeam	Ostrya virginiana	1,830,331	0.6	116,353	0.1	0.2	2.5	2.5
Eastern redbud	Cercis canadensis	5,869,940	2.1	381,267	0.2	0.6	2.6	2.4
Eastern redcedar	Juniperus virginiana	16,935,933	6.0	2,679,325	1.7	4.1	4.0	3.3
Eastern white pine	Pinus strobus	563,983	0.2	703,717	0.5	1.1	14.0	14.0
Elm	Ulmus spp.	81,296	0.0	225,470	0.1	0.3	22.0	20.0
Flowering dogwood	Cornus florida	13,946,111	4.9	1,129,979	0.7	1.7	3.1	2.2
Great leadtree	Leucaena pulverulenta	442,688	0.2	9,658	0.0	0.0	1.5	2.0
Green ash	Fraxinus pennsylvanica	3,084,067	1.1	1,029,417	0.7	1.6	5.4	3.2
Hackberry	Celtis spp.	14,837,486	5.2	2,974,206	1.9	4.6	4.4	3.0
Hawthorn	Crataegus spp.	2,000,274	0.7	57,125	0.0	0.1	1.7	1.5
Honeylocust	Gleditsia triacanthos	1,217,929	0.4	104,577	0.1	0.2	2.6	2.9
Japanese privet	Ligustrum japonicum	1,193,195	0.4	26,032	0.0	0.0	1.5	2.0
Loblolly pine	Pinus taeda	4,521,428	1.6	1,577,596	1.0	2.4	6.0	5.0
Longleaf pine	Pinus palustris	31,330	0.0	38,448	0.0	0.1	14.5	15.0
Mimosa	Albizia julibrissin	1,667,259	0.6	109,645	0.1	0.2	2.3	1.7
Mockernut hickory	Carya alba	3,703,236	1.3	618,908	0.4	0.9	3.8	3.5

continued

Table B.1—Statistics of tree species by common and scientific name, Tennessee, 2005–09 (continued)

Common name	Scientific name[a][b]	Trees	Percent of trees	Basal area			D.b.h. Average	D.b.h. Median
		- number -	*percent*	*- - ft² - -*	*ft²/ac*	*percent*	*- - - - - inches - - - - -*	
Mulberry	*Morus* spp.	516,786	0.2	11,275	0.0	0.0	1.5	2.0
Northern pin oak	*Quercus ellipsoidalis*	93,989	0.0	147,296	0.1	0.2	16.2	14.3
Northern red oak	*Quercus rubra*	534,859	0.2	827,907	0.5	1.3	14.7	10.1
Northern white cedar	*Thuja occidentalis*	31,330	0.0	4,272	0.0	0.0	4.5	5.0
Norway maple	*Acer platanoides*	71,978	0.0	21,800	0.0	0.0	6.9	6.1
Osage orange	*Maclura pomifera*	1,435,483	0.5	875,759	0.6	1.3	8.4	5.0
Other species	Other species	724,656	0.3	128,016	0.1	0.2	4.5	2.2
Pecan	*Carya illinoensis*	427,021	0.2	579,194	0.4	0.9	13.8	13.3
Pignut hickory	*Carya glabra*	4,665,525	1.6	892,371	0.6	1.4	4.0	3.5
Pin cherry	*Prunus pensylvanica*	69,690	0.0	19,005	0.0	0.0	6.5	5.0
Pin oak	*Quercus palustris*	156,649	0.1	201,807	0.1	0.3	13.7	12.6
Post oak	*Quercus stellata*	628,268	0.2	777,484	0.5	1.2	13.3	11.1
Red maple	*Acer rubrum*	9,320,200	3.3	1,861,816	1.2	2.9	4.1	3.3
Red mulberry	*Morus rubra*	719,015	0.3	122,855	0.1	0.2	3.9	1.2
Sassafras	*Sassafras albidum*	2,656,707	0.9	639,333	0.4	1.0	5.1	4.0
Scarlet oak	*Quercus coccinea*	335,689	0.1	532,231	0.3	0.8	15.0	10.1
Serviceberry	*Amelanchier arborea*	75,493	0.0	29,868	0.0	0.0	7.9	6.1
Shagbark hickory	*Carya ovata*	1,808,728	0.6	550,917	0.4	0.8	5.3	5.1
Shortleaf pine	*Pinus echinata*	1,634,528	0.6	653,836	0.4	1.0	6.4	3.1
Shumard oak	*Quercus shumardii*	93,989	0.0	452,141	0.3	0.7	28.8	29.3
Siberian elm	*Ulmus pumila*	230,320	0.1	296,763	0.2	0.5	13.6	14.0
Silver maple	*Acer saccharinum*	3,501,727	1.2	2,307,432	1.5	3.5	8.7	7.1
Slippery elm	*Ulmus rubra*	4,158,746	1.5	463,112	0.3	0.7	3.3	2.1
Smoke tree	*Cotinus coggygria*	1,328,064	0.5	28,974	0.0	0.0	1.5	2.0
Sourwood	*Oxydendrum arboreum*	4,713,749	1.7	512,749	0.3	0.8	3.4	2.1
Southern catalpa	*Catalpa bignonioides*	432,577	0.2	146,217	0.1	0.2	5.9	4.8
Southern crabapple	*Malus angustifolia*	81,296	0.0	18,845	0.0	0.0	6.0	5.0
Southern magnolia	*Magnolia grandiflora*	184,605	0.1	101,140	0.1	0.2	8.8	7.2
Southern red oak	*Quercus falcata*	1,981,270	0.7	1,936,442	1.2	3.0	9.4	7.0
Sugar maple	*Acer saccharum*	8,331,934	2.9	1,607,508	1.0	2.5	4.6	4.5
Sugarberry	*Celtis laevigata*	2,822,485	1.0	1,061,578	0.7	1.6	5.6	2.3
Swamp chestnut oak	*Quercus michauxii*	34,845	0.0	9,312	0.0	0.0	6.5	7.0
Sweet cherry	*Prunus avium*	568,589	0.2	41,923	0.0	0.1	2.9	2.8
Sweetbay	*Magnolia virginiana*	720,027	0.3	85,005	0.1	0.1	4.1	3.4
Sweetgum	*Liquidambar styraciflua*	8,247,684	2.9	2,004,271	1.3	3.1	4.3	2.2
Sycamore	*Platanus* spp.	1,082,605	0.4	385,977	0.2	0.6	5.5	1.1
Tree-of-heaven	*Ailanthus altissima*	2,387,737	0.8	155,058	0.1	0.2	2.5	2.8
Virginia pine	*Pinus virginiana*	17,081,823	6.0	2,980,906	1.9	4.6	3.8	2.3
Water oak	*Quercus nigra*	518,111	0.2	1,110,110	0.7	1.7	16.8	12.0
Weeping willow	*Salix sepulcralis*	40,648	0.0	107,303	0.1	0.2	21.5	22.0
White ash	*Fraxinus americana*	2,032,930	0.7	1,136,903	0.7	1.7	7.6	6.0
White mulberry	*Morus alba*	110,338	0.0	30,343	0.0	0.0	6.6	6.3
White oak	*Quercus alba*	2,902,649	1.0	3,233,393	2.1	5.0	10.7	7.1
Willow oak	*Quercus phellos*	184,626	0.1	497,989	0.3	0.8	17.5	13.2
Winged elm	*Ulmus alata*	9,396,010	3.3	928,162	0.6	1.4	3.1	2.2
Yellow buckeye	*Aesculus flava*	2,148,440	0.8	144,450	0.1	0.2	2.5	2.4
Yellow-poplar	*Liriodendron tulipifera*	6,317,061	2.2	4,405,342	2.8	6.8	7.9	5.0
Yellowwood	*Cladrastis lutea*	569,170	0.2	27,939	0.0	0.0	2.5	3.0

D.b.h. = Diameter at breast height.

[a] Little (1979).

[b] USDA Natural Resources Conservation Service (2011).

Appendix C—Total Species Summary

Table C.1—Total species summary, Tennessee, 2005–09

Species	Trees			Carbon storage			Carbon sequestration			Net carbon sequestration		Leaf area			Leaf biomass			Compensatory value	
	%	number	SE	%	tonnes	SE	%	tonnes	SE	tonnes	SE	%	km²	SE	%	tonnes	SE	%	dollars	SE
Chinese privet	10.4	29,676,843	10,056,460	0.8	127,541.0	35,369.2	3.1	24,907.4	7,167.3	24,697.2	7,117.4	3.1	441.6	133.9	3.6	40,148.9	12,173.1	2.0	1,594,399,254	461,720,190
Virginia pine	6.0	17,081,823	6,547,514	2.4	370,738.7	119,931.8	2.8	22,320.8	6,608.1	20,468.8	6,322.8	3.3	473.3	144.2	4.1	45,612.4	13,901.1	5.2	4,097,404,315	1,264,080,000
Eastern redcedar	6.0	16,935,933	3,617,400	2.3	348,373.0	73,644.5	2.6	20,749.5	3,907.2	19,050.2	3,955.8	4.5	647.0	130.7	16.2	179,719.9	36,292.1	4.4	3,485,710,244	720,185,410
Hackberry	5.2	14,837,485	4,936,032	4.1	622,669.2	147,407.6	5.7	45,799.8	9,967.5	43,626.0	9,516.7	6.9	991.4	214.7	5.3	58,443.9	12,653.7	5.1	4,082,528,496	891,792,471
Flowering dogwood	4.9	13,946,110	4,508,947	0.9	140,827.5	44,548.8	3.3	26,736.7	9,141.6	25,937.0	8,999.9	4.5	644.5	285.9	3.4	37,446.9	16,607.8	2.2	1,718,221,689	548,013,352
Amur honeysuckle	4.6	12,965,648	5,410,652	0.3	45,724.3	21,150.8	1.6	12,830.5	5,807.2	12,699.7	5,735.8	1.2	173.6	77.4	0.8	8,550.3	3,813.2	1.0	767,679,998	352,125,617
Winged elm	3.3	9,396,010	2,297,046	0.8	123,418.8	35,092.0	1.7	13,495.5	3,226.8	13,235.8	3,140.7	2.8	399.1	99.2	2.6	28,834.3	7,164.4	1.5	1,206,349,547	303,288,806
Red maple	3.3	9,320,200	2,779,948	2.8	438,004.4	113,902.7	3.4	27,251.4	5,725.8	26,389.3	5,544.0	4.3	616.8	138.3	3.7	41,538.3	9,313.9	3.9	3,063,829,401	661,188,424
Black tupelo	3.1	8,746,939	3,203,396	1.1	169,803.1	46,076.1	1.7	13,680.0	4,622.3	12,510.3	4,741.2	2.1	305.2	99.7	1.0	10,557.5	3,449.3	1.7	1,361,833,562	408,445,250
American beech	3.0	8,665,227	4,791,447	0.7	103,428.2	64,925.7	1.5	12,510.3	6,219.5	11,928.0	6,179.5	3.0	430.6	229.3	1.7	18,348.0	9,769.2	1.1	869,053,416	436,122,810
Sugar maple	2.9	8,331,934	2,472,024	2.5	387,142.2	101,872.3	3.7	29,654.1	6,591.1	15,059.5	15,137.4	4.1	588.7	132.8	3.2	35,465.3	7,998.3	2.4	1,913,572,615	438,572,847
Sweetgum	2.9	8,247,683	3,079,922	2.8	436,947.1	143,325.9	2.2	18,088.7	5,158.1	17,057.5	4,999.2	2.1	301.8	86.5	1.2	13,853.1	3,970.4	2.6	2,070,850,518	599,666,453
Black locust	2.8	7,906,797	3,815,428	1.4	214,538.7	61,139.2	1.4	11,375.6	3,691.9	2,996.7	6,393.6	1.2	175.5	74.6	0.9	9,446.0	4,018.3	0.7	550,740,957	165,114,663
Black cherry	2.7	7,808,122	1,943,060	2.3	355,338.7	102,553.6	3.2	25,992.0	5,523.8	24,611.7	5,212.0	2.4	350.4	77.9	2.5	27,177.5	6,044.0	2.3	1,832,706,824	391,347,706
Yellow-poplar	2.2	6,317,062	1,932,250	6.5	996,833.6	253,774.7	4.3	34,487.3	7,831.5	33,098.0	7,485.8	5.4	783.9	175.0	4.2	46,209.7	10,313.8	7.2	5,733,394,506	1,333,250,000
Eastern redbud	2.1	5,869,940	2,327,224	0.3	47,506.3	15,264.9	1.1	9,018.3	3,229.0	8,760.1	3,170.4	0.8	109.3	37.4	0.6	6,999.8	2,394.9	0.8	616,125,039	202,798,581
American elm	1.8	5,154,064	1,579,130	1.0	160,407.1	52,430.6	1.2	9,835.1	2,469.1	9,196.5	2,403.0	2.1	305.0	80.9	2.0	22,185.3	5,884.1	1.3	1,046,050,255	278,018,032
Chestnut oak	1.8	5,099,711	1,479,177	9.9	1,517,390.7	510,472.6	7.2	57,954.5	18,229.2	56,878.7	17,873.1	3.9	558.0	158.6	4.0	43,855.8	12,462.2	5.3	4,210,349,474	1,329,340,000
Sourwood	1.7	4,713,748	2,345,623	0.5	78,091.7	23,317.1	1.0	8,045.4	2,582.7	6,613.9	2,733.8	0.9	124.4	41.7	0.3	3,785.5	1,268.9	0.8	634,603,727	188,187,404
Pignut hickory	1.6	4,665,525	2,365,725	1.4	211,267.5	117,041.5	1.5	12,310.8	4,744.1	11,936.4	4,607.2	1.3	186.2	72.0	0.3	3,548.3	1,372.0	1.4	1,123,707,832	439,905,933
Loblolly pine	1.6	4,521,428	2,171,322	1.3	207,234.1	90,802.7	1.3	10,879.0	5,014.7	10,487.3	4,916.9	1.7	244.0	96.4	1.8	19,793.2	7,819.1	3.4	2,698,401,384	1,122,570,000
Slippery elm	1.5	4,158,747	1,216,957	0.4	64,512.5	22,358.8	0.7	5,721.4	1,577.7	4,926.3	1,623.2	1.4	201.7	76.1	0.8	9,029.2	3,405.7	0.6	472,551,186	122,902,829
Boxelder	1.4	3,918,957	1,439,175	2.2	340,001.1	95,135.8	2.1	16,956.3	4,016.8	15,376.2	3,497.8	2.2	314.5	78.2	2.6	28,769.4	7,157.2	1.2	978,982,273	241,464,970
Mockernut hickory	1.3	3,703,236	1,365,958	0.9	134,258.4	45,148.0	1.3	10,180.7	3,201.2	9,586.4	3,100.2	1.0	137.1	40.9	0.6	7,187.3	2,143.2	1.1	889,642,333	274,410,275
Silver maple	1.2	3,501,727	1,106,034	4.5	688,402.7	170,181.1	3.6	28,953.7	7,831.7	21,593.6	7,692.2	3.3	471.9	121.0	2.2	24,836.3	6,368.0	2.2	1,787,210,064	488,550,125
Green ash	1.1	3,084,068	1,037,074	1.7	261,891.7	135,319.9	1.3	10,147.2	4,376.1	7,514.1	4,857.1	1.7	238.3	86.5	1.4	15,542.4	5,644.9	1.1	873,466,927	382,581,371
White oak	1.0	2,902,648	853,179	4.8	737,708.1	252,158.3	3.3	26,379.7	7,496.4	24,495.4	7,150.9	1.9	268.5	74.3	1.8	19,530.5	5,408.4	4.0	3,196,868,170	923,207,787
Sugarberry	1.0	2,822,485	1,485,572	1.8	270,021.7	106,068.6	1.6	12,871.2	4,589.1	11,164.2	3,982.9	2.4	346.5	127.2	2.1	23,558.9	8,649.2	1.5	1,168,761,063	429,863,266
Sassafras	0.9	2,656,708	910,641	0.9	132,102.5	43,820.4	0.8	6,356.1	1,912.2	4,476.4	1,952.6	0.7	96.1	32.6	0.4	4,728.2	1,604.2	0.7	559,937,722	163,397,040
Callery pear	0.9	2,445,969	1,054,092	0.3	50,509.7	22,494.3	0.9	6,951.2	2,923.2	6,748.8	2,840.9	0.5	76.4	29.7	0.5	5,678.8	2,204.6	0.8	617,426,312	265,392,924
Tree-of-heaven	0.8	2,387,737	1,770,075	0.2	24,681.7	12,102.7	0.3	2,618.0	1,403.0	2,588.0	1,390.8	0.4	63.2	38.9	0.4	4,691.4	2,890.7	0.1	97,727,314	43,185,746
Common persimmon	0.8	2,239,172	1,392,217	0.2	32,768.6	12,302.3	0.5	3,978.5	1,755.3	3,911.2	1,737.8	0.5	68.7	36.3	0.5	5,104.5	2,696.5	0.4	305,574,468	113,422,114
Yellow buckeye	0.8	2,148,441	2,068,740	0.1	21,947.3	15,695.4	0.3	2,684.7	2,166.2	2,666.6	2,154.9	0.4	61.9	51.5	0.4	4,033.0	3,355.6	0.2	130,597,738	96,287,338
White ash	0.7	2,032,930	715,791	2.0	313,263.2	120,401.5	1.8	14,818.8	5,284.3	14,033.1	4,978.6	1.3	188.2	71.1	1.0	10,695.4	4,039.5	1.6	1,302,416,537	477,697,631
Hawthorn	0.7	2,000,274	1,581,528	0.0	6,622.5	5,459.1	0.2	1,659.9	1,408.6	1,652.3	1,402.1	0.3	42.6	35.0	0.1	1,532.9	1,257.6	0.1	91,733,107	69,959,043
Southern red oak	0.7	1,981,270	963,289	4.6	700,423.0	413,341.0	3.0	24,186.3	13,544.6	22,102.9	12,058.7	1.6	229.2	104.5	1.6	17,874.1	8,145.4	3.2	2,554,638,566	1,453,500,000
Eastern hophornbeam	0.6	1,830,330	1,062,487	0.1	11,096.3	6,631.8	0.3	2,332.0	1,409.3	2,303.0	1,386.8	0.9	126.3	73.7	0.7	8,244.5	4,814.1	0.2	175,381,418	98,808,530
Shagbark hickory	0.6	1,808,728	973,195	0.9	133,112.8	52,098.4	0.8	6,472.2	2,476.7	5,425.9	2,599.8	0.7	105.7	50.3	0.7	7,740.0	3,680.2	0.8	619,367,494	243,269,408

continued

Table C.1—Total species summary, Tennessee, 2005–09 (continued)

Species	Trees - number -	- SE -	%	Carbon storage - tonnes -	- SE -	%	Carbon sequestration - tonnes -	- SE -	%	Net carbon sequestration - tonnes -	- SE -	%	Leaf area - km²	SE	%	Leaf biomass - tonnes -	- SE -	%	Compensatory value - dollars -	- SE -
Mimosa	1,667,258	1,093,781	0.6	16,694.6	8,589.8	0.1	2,577.5	1,189.5	0.3	2,521.2	1,160.5	0.3	45.8	25.6	0.2	1,992.1	1,111.7	0.3	214,554,049	100,668,069
Shortleaf pine	1,634,528	944,211	0.6	77,305.0	35,856.8	0.5	2,736.5	1,370.1	0.3	1,718.5	1,308.4	0.4	60.8	33.4	0.5	5,861.8	3,223.4	0.6	444,834,642	217,130,383
Osage orange	1,435,483	793,491	0.5	227,830.3	140,065.0	1.5	10,063.8	5,536.8	1.2	8,212.4	4,871.2	2.2	237.6	127.5	1.6	23,888.1	12,819.0	1.3	1,004,460,247	563,415,887
Cockspur hawthorn	1,432,599	1,332,170	0.5	10,290.2	7,552.6	0.1	1,501.2	1,113.5	0.2	1,491.9	1,107.3	0.1	11.3	8.0	0.1	847.6	603.3	0.1	117,164,471	82,934,710
Smoke tree	1,328,064	1,328,063	0.5	1,674.6	1,674.6	0.0	704.2	704.2	0.1	701.9	701.9	0.1	7.4	7.4	0.0	550.8	550.8	0.1	44,585,013	44,584,963
Black walnut	1,247,642	412,243	0.4	241,595.7	68,061.6	1.6	10,255.8	2,605.5	1.3	8,729.8	2,638.2	1.6	231.3	62.9	1.7	18,537.1	5,037.8	1.5	1,212,151,445	316,394,982
Honeylocust	1,217,929	1,139,751	0.4	19,160.3	14,544.7	0.1	1,592.5	1,055.6	0.2	1,577.2	1,046.8	0.2	16.8	12.7	0.1	1,761.2	1,334.6	0.2	137,677,297	87,253,006
Japanese privet	1,193,195	1,193,194	0.4	2,292.9	2,292.9	0.0	1,110.2	1,110.2	0.1	1,092.2	1,092.2	0.0	1.4	1.4	0.0	124.4	124.4	0.1	60,085,896	60,085,820
Black oak	1,165,417	309,910	0.4	391,550.1	112,626.2	2.5	16,080.1	4,367.9	2.0	14,923.9	4,214.4	1.1	153.5	49.0	1.0	10,847.9	3,464.2	1.5	1,192,435,798	322,854,992
Sycamore	1,082,606	621,071	0.4	94,936.1	45,283.2	0.6	4,861.5	1,883.2	0.6	4,609.5	1,778.5	0.8	119.5	51.4	0.5	5,487.7	2,360.4	0.6	496,615,789	203,334,043
Chinkapin oak	1,041,915	489,212	0.4	162,522.0	88,199.0	1.1	7,504.5	2,840.4	0.9	7,270.8	2,750.3	0.7	98.7	46.0	0.8	9,059.4	4,225.7	0.9	678,289,205	258,927,924
Common cherry laurel	889,453	800,996	0.3	19,765.1	18,281.9	0.1	2,093.4	1,522.7	0.3	2,008.4	1,454.5	0.1	14.9	11.8	0.1	1,150.9	916.6	0.2	157,058,676	123,666,785
Bitternut hickory	860,180	497,146	0.3	131,788.9	95,989.3	0.9	5,969.7	3,450.2	0.7	5,857.1	3,383.0	0.6	108.9	59.6	0.8	6,845.9	3,748.3	0.7	581,431,354	331,687,908
Other species	724,656	489,534	0.3	21,125.9	14,662.2	0.1	2,540.1	1,628.5	0.3	2,458.0	1,570.1	0.1	20.6	13.9	0.1	1,527.6	1,031.0	0.3	256,524,159	175,613,144
Sweetbay	720,027	555,314	0.3	12,132.6	8,582.0	0.1	2,731.8	1,965.0	0.3	2,676.4	1,926.4	0.2	21.7	15.5	0.1	3,107.6	2,208.4	0.3	228,572,746	161,867,281
Red mulberry	719,015	459,668	0.3	24,453.3	13,376.0	0.2	1,934.2	1,053.3	0.2	1,840.5	1,005.8	0.3	45.3	23.9	0.4	4,496.8	2,372.3	0.2	174,304,269	103,912,182
Post oak	628,269	212,845	0.2	254,284.2	131,135.9	1.7	8,269.6	3,208.5	1.0	5,627.0	2,290.0	0.7	102.2	39.4	0.8	8,698.4	3,355.2	0.7	532,897,482	192,918,269
Yellowwood	569,170	569,170	0.2	1,998.6	1,998.6	0.0	530.4	530.4	0.1	517.1	517.1	0.0	2.9	2.9	0.0	214.7	214.7	0.1	47,844,815	47,844,773
Sweet cherry	568,589	509,794	0.2	6,606.1	4,671.4	0.0	1,488.4	1,122.3	0.2	1,451.6	1,095.9	0.1	20.6	15.4	0.1	1,590.8	1,190.9	0.1	89,086,817	63,539,972
Eastern white pine	563,982	335,127	0.2	93,854.8	73,833.7	0.6	3,538.5	2,470.5	0.4	2,958.0	2,176.5	0.6	82.7	60.4	0.5	5,318.9	3,884.1	1.7	1,348,673,584	1,089,770,000
Northern red oak	534,860	206,135	0.2	270,543.0	133,355.0	1.8	8,161.4	3,333.3	1.0	7,654.0	3,106.6	0.7	97.6	38.1	0.7	7,774.0	3,035.4	0.8	620,684,370	253,742,037
Water oak	518,111	367,543	0.2	440,549.4	214,892.0	2.9	13,139.7	6,372.5	1.6	8,827.1	4,168.0	0.7	96.7	43.4	0.8	9,141.6	4,100.0	1.7	1,388,109,544	658,420,326
Mulberry	516,786	516,786	0.2	593.5	593.5	0.0	376.4	376.4	0.0	371.3	371.3	0.0	8.4	8.4	0.1	710.0	710.0	0.0	26,023,870	26,023,845
Common plum	477,533	444,057	0.2	1,856.6	1,429.3	0.0	386.5	284.3	0.0	384.8	283.2	0.0	4.0	3.0	0.0	310.8	232.3	0.0	24,795,812	17,876,048
Great leadtree	442,688	442,688	0.2	289.5	289.5	0.0	166.9	166.9	0.0	166.5	166.5	0.0	2.2	2.2	0.0	165.5	165.5	0.0	14,861,671	14,861,654
Southern catalpa	432,577	399,255	0.2	34,543.6	29,158.0	0.2	1,626.7	1,152.0	0.2	1,602.2	1,135.3	0.1	14.5	10.3	0.1	772.8	547.4	0.2	135,468,062	97,060,711
Pecan	427,021	150,873	0.2	181,909.5	86,435.7	1.0	7,999.4	3,286.2	1.0	7,310.8	2,962.7	0.7	98.0	46.5	0.6	6,811.6	3,235.2	1.1	853,141,366	359,236,253
Cherrybark oak	414,522	180,525	0.1	353,739.3	162,629.3	2.3	10,139.3	4,616.4	1.3	9,670.7	4,380.1	0.8	122.5	55.3	1.2	13,815.4	6,235.1	1.2	988,661,312	454,903,880
Baldcypress	337,903	185,630	0.1	89,728.3	72,427.5	0.6	2,599.0	1,733.3	0.3	2,518.5	1,681.6	0.8	115.5	85.7	0.8	12,753.6	9,461.6	1.2	556,423,837	384,462,098
Scarlet oak	335,689	153,496	0.1	177,659.8	130,637.9	1.2	5,469.7	3,242.7	0.7	4,668.1	2,810.9	0.5	65.0	38.7	0.4	4,735.6	2,816.7	0.4	997,575,798	756,947,558
Black willow	324,164	150,190	0.1	44,677.2	28,581.6	0.3	2,060.3	1,139.7	0.3	1,878.7	1,079.5	0.4	60.5	29.7	0.3	3,733.9	1,836.1	1.3	173,331,451	97,903,277
Eastern cottonwood	277,026	143,952	0.1	114,481.2	99,188.1	0.7	4,215.7	3,371.2	0.5	3,820.3	2,993.5	0.4	59.6	32.7	0.4	4,296.8	2,360.8	0.4	280,320,911	204,263,441
Siberian elm	230,320	201,439	0.1	68,573.0	48,698.0	0.4	3,053.8	2,298.4	0.4	2,786.9	2,114.9	0.4	42.1	30.0	0.3	2,866.3	2,043.8	0.4	281,848,079	233,264,308
Willow oak	184,626	82,611	0.1	188,857.6	138,990.8	1.2	4,249.4	2,716.1	0.5	3,581.2	2,203.3	0.3	87.5	60.8	0.6	7,765.8	5,396.8	1.1	840,993,645	561,379,684
Southern magnolia	184,604	129,636	0.1	22,407.5	18,175.5	0.1	1,655.9	1,229.1	0.2	1,566.2	1,157.1	0.2	12.9	10.3	0.1	1,747.0	1,391.4	0.3	217,648,977	164,854,842
Pin oak	156,649	81,375	0.1	65,527.3	50,113.8	0.4	2,983.2	1,964.7	0.4	2,727.9	1,772.8	0.2	31.1	18.6	0.2	2,816.2	1,687.1	0.3	215,475,179	132,664,870
Blackjack oak	139,379	139,377	0.0	9,577.3	9,577.1	0.1	735.0	734.9	0.1	728.0	728.0	0.0	5.1	5.1	0.0	471.6	471.6	0.1	59,832,806	59,831,947
Buttermut	134,230	134,229	0.0	37,891.2	37,890.7	0.2	1,068.3	1,068.3	0.1	1,041.9	1,041.9	0.2	24.1	24.1	0.1	1,328.8	1,328.8	0.1	71,401,668	71,400,870

continued

Table C.1—Total species summary, Tennessee, 2005–09 (continued)

Species	Trees - number -	%	- SE - -	%	Carbon storage - tonnes -	- - SE - -	%	Carbon sequestration tonnes	- SE -	%	Net carbon sequestration - tonnes -	- SE -	%	Leaf area km²	SE	%	Leaf biomass - tonnes -	- SE - -	%	Compensatory value - - dollars - -	- - - SE - - -
Cherry	121,094	0.0	90,514	0.1	13,376.0	11,362.9	0.2	1,284.0	1,034.9	0.2	1,229.3	988.9	0.1	12.0	11.4	0.1	928.5	881.6	0.1	111,893,341	87,382,764
White mulberry	110,338	0.0	80,677	0.0	4,877.7	3,460.3	0.1	438.1	313.7	0.1	434.5	311.2	0.1	7.8	5.8	0.1	573.7	424.3	0.1	47,266,779	33,636,318
Blue ash	104,535	0.0	104,533	0.1	10,089.1	10,089.0	0.1	597.9	597.9	0.1	590.6	590.6	0.1	8.4	8.4	0.1	677.2	677.2	0.1	60,585,806	60,584,937
Chinese chestnut	97,504	0.0	71,695	0.1	9,908.0	7,478.0	0.1	819.6	645.7	0.1	789.7	618.9	0.1	8.7	7.1	0.1	608.2	498.5	0.1	84,278,654	66,234,990
Crabapple	93,989	0.0	93,988	0.0	4,911.8	4,911.8	0.1	621.1	621.1	0.1	600.5	600.5	0.0	5.5	5.5	0.0	473.8	473.8	0.1	64,837,529	64,836,494
Northern pin oak	93,989	0.0	69,659	0.3	46,886.4	33,499.2	0.3	2,099.8	1,474.6	0.3	1,917.3	1,347.2	0.1	17.9	13.5	0.1	1,841.0	1,388.4	0.3	225,448,809	158,307,423
Shumard oak	93,989	0.0	53,494	1.3	197,413.5	119,509.6	0.7	5,812.6	3,450.0	0.7	5,055.4	2,993.1	0.2	33.2	19.5	0.3	3,048.7	1,791.6	1.0	784,088,421	465,617,049
Southern crabapple	81,296	0.0	81,295	0.0	2,657.3	2,657.3	0.0	269.5	269.5	0.0	265.8	265.8	0.0	3.9	3.9	0.0	332.0	332.0	0.0	25,033,755	25,033,447
Elm	81,296	0.0	81,295	0.4	56,447.2	56,446.5	0.2	1,912.1	1,912.1	0.2	1,694.7	1,694.7	0.1	8.8	8.8	0.1	601.7	601.7	0.3	262,962,780	262,959,545
Serviceberry	75,493	0.0	53,538	0.0	6,081.9	4,526.3	0.0	257.9	257.9	0.0	47.3	320.8	0.0	3.0	3.0	0.0	228.4	228.4	0.0	30,352,993	30,352,620
Norway maple	71,978	0.0	51,320	0.0	4,266.5	3,034.0	0.0	397.1	281.5	0.0	387.4	274.5	0.0	5.6	4.1	0.0	300.0	219.1	0.1	43,039,872	30,529,796
Pin cherry	69,690	0.0	69,689	0.0	3,406.0	3,405.9	0.0	134.7	134.7	0.0	29.8	29.8	0.0	2.0	2.0	0.0	98.7	98.7	0.0	10,279,651	10,279,503
Dahoon	62,660	0.0	62,659	0.0	2,217.7	2,217.6	0.0	331.0	331.0	0.0	321.5	321.5	0.0	1.9	1.9	0.0	249.0	249.0	0.0	32,556,558	32,556,039
American holly	62,660	0.0	62,659	0.0	6,210.8	6,210.7	0.0	385.8	385.8	0.0	381.3	381.3	0.0	6.4	6.4	0.1	857.6	857.6	0.1	39,748,617	39,747,983
Weeping willow	40,648	0.0	40,648	0.2	33,101.1	33,100.7	0.1	1,156.4	1,156.4	0.1	1,133.2	1,133.2	0.1	13.2	13.2	0.1	813.5	813.5	0.1	105,144,942	105,143,649
Black birch	34,845	0.0	34,844	0.0	7,295.3	7,295.2	0.0	388.7	388.7	0.0	383.5	383.5	0.0	1.9	1.9	0.0	113.6	113.6	0.0	29,714,750	29,714,323
Swamp chestnut oak	34,845	0.0	34,844	0.0	1,795.4	1,795.4	0.0	160.8	160.8	0.0	159.4	159.4	0.0	4.5	4.5	0.0	273.8	273.8	0.0	17,338,183	17,337,934
American basswood	34,845	0.0	34,844	0.0	1,503.2	1,503.1	0.0	114.3	114.3	0.0	113.3	113.2	0.0	4.4	4.4	0.0	127.0	127.0	0.0	18,680,627	18,680,359
Eastern hemlock	34,845	0.0	34,844	0.0	1,075.4	1,075.4	0.0	83.1	83.1	0.0	82.3	82.3	0.0	4.7	4.7	0.0	437.4	437.4	0.0	16,263,005	16,262,772
Longleaf pine	31,330	0.0	31,329	0.0	4,545.0	4,544.9	0.0	197.8	197.8	0.0	180.1	180.1	0.0	4.1	4.1	0.0	393.0	393.0	0.1	77,440,689	77,439,453
Bur oak	31,330	0.0	31,329	0.1	8,739.4	8,739.3	0.1	490.3	490.3	0.1	455.9	455.9	0.0	4.5	4.5	0.0	417.2	417.2	0.1	68,834,850	68,833,752
Northern white cedar	31,330	0.0	31,329	0.0	536.6	536.6	0.0	58.3	58.3	0.0	56.1	56.1	0.0	2.4	2.4	0.0	463.1	463.1	0.0	10,973,769	10,973,594
Carolina hemlock	31,330	0.0	31,329	0.0	1,309.0	1,309.0	0.0	115.5	115.5	0.0	110.2	110.2	0.0	7.2	7.2	0.0	499.2	499.2	0.0	27,624,160	27,623,719

SE = standard error.

Appendix D—Tree Species Statistics by Land Use

Table D.1—Tree statistics by land use and species, Tennessee, 2005–09

Land use and species	Trees (number)	Basal area (ft²/ac)	D.b.h. Average (inches)	D.b.h. Median (inches)
Agriculture				
American elm	583,665	0.3	3.2	2.6
Black cherry	806,592	1.3	6.2	4.9
Black locust	260,082	0.5	7.4	6.8
Boxelder	520,164	1.4	8.6	7.5
Cherrybark oak	111,464	1.1	17.5	15.5
Chinese privet	1,453,757	0.6	3.0	2.5
Common persimmon	37,155	0.0	5.5	5.5
Eastern redcedar	1,464,565	1.3	4.2	3.6
Flowering dogwood	546,510	0.2	3.0	2.6
Green ash	185,773	0.7	10.1	8.5
Hackberry	4,111,996	2.0	2.9	1.9
Red mulberry	37,155	0.2	11.5	11.5
Sassafras	334,391	0.5	6.9	6.7
Silver maple	148,618	0.9	14.3	14.5
Southern red oak	148,618	1.7	17.0	10.0
Sugar maple	111,464	0.2	7.2	6.7
Sugarberry	37,155	0.0	5.5	5.5
Sweetgum	620,819	0.6	3.5	1.7
Virginia pine	371,546	0.9	8.4	7.0
Willow oak	37,155	0.2	13.5	13.5
Winged elm	2,000,266	0.6	2.3	1.6
Yellow-poplar	260,082	1.3	11.5	8.8
Commercial/industrial				
Black walnut	79,596	0.1	6.0	6.0
Black willow	79,596	0.2	7.0	6.0
Boxelder	79,596	1.4	21.0	14.0
Cherry	39,798	0.1	6.5	6.5
Eastern redbud	119,394	0.1	5.5	5.5
Eastern redcedar	585,525	0.5	4.7	4.6
Hackberry	278,586	0.6	7.1	6.5
Hawthorn	1,557,586	0.3	1.9	1.8
Loblolly pine	198,990	0.8	10.3	10.3
Mimosa	1,011,858	0.1	1.5	1.5
Pecan	39,798	1.0	27.5	27.5
Red maple	39,798	0.0	5.5	5.5
Siberian elm	198,990	1.1	11.7	14.5
Commercial/industrial (continued)				
Silver maple	39,798	0.6	21.5	21.5
Slippery elm	545,727	0.1	1.2	0.0
Sourwood	39,798	0.1	9.5	9.5
Sugar maple	119,394	0.9	13.5	14.5
Sweet cherry	505,929	0.2	2.5	2.5
Sweetgum	585,525	1.0	3.3	0.0
Virginia pine	39,798	0.0	5.5	5.5
Winged elm	39,798	0.1	7.5	7.5
Forest				
American basswood	34,845	0.1	7.5	7.5
American beech	8,445,918	1.2	1.8	1.6
American elm	2,223,735	1.4	3.1	1.6
Amur honeysuckle	7,525,697	1.2	2.0	1.9
Baldcypress	243,914	1.9	16.6	18.5
Bitternut hickory	721,447	1.6	7.3	3.8
Black birch	34,845	0.1	11.5	11.5
Black cherry	6,123,984	3.3	3.7	3.0
Black locust	7,009,360	2.6	2.8	1.9
Black oak	801,432	3.4	12.2	10.5
Black tupelo	5,974,309	3.0	3.2	2.2
Black walnut	557,518	1.5	9.7	9.0
Black willow	69,690	0.4	15.5	15.5
Blackjack oak	139,379	0.2	7.3	7.0
Blue ash	104,535	0.2	8.8	8.7
Boxelder	1,198,980	0.6	3.4	2.4
Callery pear	442,688	0.1	2.5	2.5
Cherrybark oak	209,069	2.2	19.0	22.0
Chestnut oak	4,652,580	13.5	8.5	6.6
Chinese chestnut	34,845	0.1	8.5	8.5
Chinese privet	18,592,899	2.1	1.7	1.6
Chinkapin oak	825,981	0.9	5.7	3.9
Cockspur hawthorn	1,432,599	0.3	2.0	1.6
Common persimmon	174,224	0.3	7.9	7.8
Common plum	477,533	0.1	1.8	1.5
Eastern cottonwood	69,690	0.2	9.0	6.0
Eastern hemlock	34,845	0.0	6.5	6.5
Forest (continued)				
Eastern hophornbeam	1,432,599	0.3	2.0	1.6
Eastern redbud	2,317,975	0.5	2.1	1.9
Eastern redcedar	10,223,006	5.8	3.5	2.7
Eastern white pine	34,845	0.2	13.5	13.5
Flowering dogwood	2,725,818	0.5	2.2	2.0
Great leadtree	442,688	0.0	1.5	1.5
Green ash	1,955,271	2.8	5.3	3.2
Hackberry	7,079,050	4.0	4.0	3.5
Hawthorn	442,688	0.0	0.8	0.0
Honeylocust	34,845	0.0	6.5	6.5
Loblolly pine	3,746,614	3.2	4.7	4.2
Mimosa	69,690	0.1	6.0	6.0
Mockernut hickory	2,363,115	1.2	3.4	2.7
Northern red oak	418,138	2.4	13.4	10.8
Osage orange	557,518	2.0	11.0	11.0
Other species	442,688	0.1	2.5	2.5
Pecan	104,535	0.2	7.5	7.5
Pignut hickory	4,004,783	3.0	3.8	3.2
Pin cherry	69,690	0.1	6.5	6.0
Post oak	452,983	2.6	13.7	11.5
Red maple	7,755,356	4.5	3.6	3.2
Red mulberry	547,223	0.1	2.3	1.6
Sassafras	1,313,809	2.1	6.9	5.8
Scarlet oak	174,224	0.7	12.3	10.8
Serviceberry	34,845	0.1	9.5	9.5
Shagbark hickory	1,442,894	1.8	4.7	1.6
Shortleaf pine	1,512,583	2.2	5.9	3.7
Silver maple	1,024,755	0.3	2.6	2.2
Slippery elm	3,004,577	1.4	3.4	3.2
Smoke tree	1,328,064	0.1	1.5	1.5
Sourwood	4,552,006	1.9	3.3	2.7
Southern catalpa	34,845	0.4	21.5	21.5
Southern red oak	1,303,514	1.7	4.8	1.7
Sugar maple	4,611,400	2.3	3.7	4.2
Sugarberry	1,711,357	1.7	4.5	2.6
Swamp chestnut oak	34,845	0.0	6.5	6.5

continued

Table D.1—Tree species statistics by land use (continued)

Land use and species	Trees (number)	Basal area (ft²/ac)	D.b.h. Average (inches)	D.b.h. Median (inches)
Forest (continued)				
Sweetgum	5,412,832	4.9	4.0	1.9
Sycamore	69,690	0.1	7.5	6.0
Tree-of-heaven	442,688	0.0	1.5	1.5
Virginia pine	3,596,939	3.4	4.3	2.5
Water oak	34,845	1.2	37.5	29.0
White ash	1,209,275	2.7	7.7	8.2
White mulberry	69,690	0.1	6.0	6.0
White oak	2,104,946	8.2	9.1	6.5
Willow oak	34,845	0.1	7.5	7.5
Winged elm	5,238,608	2.4	3.2	2.5
Yellow-poplar	4,478,356	13.6	8.1	5.1
Other urban				
American elm	671,150	1.2	7.3	6.1
Bitternut hickory	44,743	0.1	9.5	9.5
Black cherry	178,973	0.3	6.8	6.0
Black locust	89,487	0.2	8.0	8.0
Black oak	44,743	0.4	17.5	17.5
Black tupelo	44,743	0.3	14.5	14.5
Black willow	134,230	0.2	6.2	5.7
Boxelder	357,947	1.0	9.3	7.0
Butternut	134,230	0.6	12.5	11.7
Callery pear	569,170	0.4	4.5	4.5
Chinese privet	4,866,567	1.5	2.7	2.4
Common persimmon	1,138,341	0.4	3.0	3.0
Eastern cottonwood	44,743	0.1	7.5	7.5
Eastern redcedar	402,690	0.7	7.3	7.5
Eastern white pine	313,204	2.5	16.6	15.8
Flowering dogwood	2,321,425	1.2	3.8	4.0
Green ash	178,973	0.2	5.8	5.7
Hackberry	1,285,064	1.7	5.0	5.4
Honeylocust	1,183,084	0.5	2.5	2.0
Northern red oak	44,743	0.6	22.5	22.5
Osage orange	658,657	0.5	4.2	3.6
Pecan	44,743	0.4	17.5	17.5
Scarlet oak	89,487	1.6	25.5	22.0
Silver maple	939,611	1.9	8.0	7.1

Land use and species	Trees (number)	Basal area (ft²/ac)	D.b.h. Average (inches)	D.b.h. Median (inches)
Other urban (continued)				
Slippery elm	44,743	0.0	5.5	5.5
Southern red oak	313,204	4.7	22.6	25.2
Sugar maple	44,743	0.1	6.5	6.5
Sweetgum	927,117	1.7	6.3	2.8
Sycamore	837,630	1.0	4.1	1.7
Tree-of-heaven	1,841,741	0.5	2.5	2.3
Virginia pine	89,487	0.9	19.5	18.0
Water oak	357,947	1.4	11.3	11.5
Winged elm	927,117	0.7	4.2	2.8
Yellow-poplar	44,743	0.2	13.5	13.5
Yellowwood	569,170	0.1	2.5	2.5
Residential				
American beech	219,308	0.6	12.2	11.5
American elm	1,077,431	0.7	3.9	1.7
American holly	62,660	0.1	9.0	9.0
Amur honeysuckle	4,406,379	0.5	1.9	1.6
Baldcypress	93,989	0.1	8.8	8.7
Bitternut hickory	93,989	0.2	10.5	10.5
Black cherry	657,925	1.3	10.1	8.5
Black locust	344,627	0.8	10.9	8.6
Black oak	156,649	0.2	8.9	7.5
Black tupelo	62,660	0.2	11.5	7.0
Black walnut	407,287	1.1	12.5	12.8
Boxelder	1,193,195	0.1	1.8	1.7
Bur oak	31,330	0.1	13.5	13.5
Callery pear	156,649	0.2	9.1	7.5
Carolina hemlock	31,330	0.0	7.5	7.5
Cherrybark oak	93,989	0.5	18.2	18.5
Chinese chestnut	62,660	0.1	9.5	9.0
Chinese privet	1,622,257	0.3	2.6	2.0
Chinkapin oak	93,989	0.3	13.8	12.5
Common cherry laurel	889,452	0.2	2.5	1.6
Common persimmon	889,452	0.2	2.2	1.6
Crabapple	93,989	0.1	6.8	6.5
Dahoon holly	62,660	0.0	5.5	5.0
Eastern hophornbeam	397,732	0.1	4.5	4.5

Land use and species	Trees (number)	Basal area (ft²/ac)	D.b.h. Average (inches)	D.b.h. Median (inches)
Residential (continued)				
Eastern redbud	1,841,565	0.5	3.7	3.3
Eastern redcedar	648,370	0.5	4.9	1.8
Eastern white pine	93,989	0.1	6.8	6.5
Flowering dogwood	3,892,883	1.0	3.3	2.8
Green ash	125,319	0.4	14.0	14.0
Hackberry	1,838,901	3.1	8.7	7.9
Japanese privet	1,193,195	0.1	1.5	1.5
Loblolly pine	250,638	0.8	12.9	14.0
Longleaf pine	31,330	0.1	14.5	14.5
Mimosa	585,711	0.2	3.3	1.7
Mockernut hickory	62,660	0.3	18.0	16.0
Northern pin oak	93,989	0.4	16.2	14.5
Northern red oak	31,330	0.3	25.5	25.5
Northern white cedar	31,330	0.0	4.5	4.5
Norway maple	31,330	0.0	7.5	7.5
Osage orange	219,308	0.8	14.1	13.5
Other species	281,968	0.3	7.7	7.5
Pecan	156,649	0.4	11.9	12.5
Pignut hickory	62,660	0.1	8.0	7.0
Pin oak	156,649	0.6	13.7	12.5
Post oak	93,989	0.3	13.8	15.5
Red maple	805,019	1.9	9.8	6.1
Red mulberry	93,989	0.1	9.5	8.7
Sassafras	491,721	0.1	2.7	1.6
Scarlet oak	31,330	0.0	8.5	8.5
Shumard oak	93,989	1.2	28.8	29.0
Siberian elm	31,330	0.3	25.5	25.5
Silver maple	657,925	2.9	15.9	14.5
Slippery elm	523,051	0.3	4.4	2.7
Southern catalpa	397,732	0.1	4.5	4.5
Southern magnolia	62,660	0.1	7.5	7.0
Southern red oak	93,989	0.2	10.5	5.7
Sugar maple	1,610,037	1.8	6.7	5.1
Sugarberry	313,298	1.1	14.2	15.0
Sweet cherry	62,660	0.0	6.5	6.0
Sweetgum	62,660	0.1	8.5	8.5

continued

Table D.1—Tree species statistics by land use (continued)

Land use and species	Trees (number)	Basal area (ft²/ac)	D.b.h. Average (inches)	Median (inches)
Residential (continued)				
Sycamore	93,989	0.2	11.2	9.5
Tree-of-heaven	62,660	0.1	7.5	7.0
Virginia pine	4,895,435	2.1	4.1	3.4
Water oak	125,319	1.5	26.8	21.0
White ash	742,359	1.3	7.7	1.9
White oak	187,979	1.8	23.3	24.0
Willow oak	31,330	0.9	43.5	29.0
Winged elm	156,649	0.1	6.1	5.8
Yellow-poplar	1,046,101	1.5	4.9	1.7
Transportation				
American elm	598,082	0.1	2.1	1.6
Amur honeysuckle	1,033,572	0.1	2.0	2.0
Black cherry	40,648	0.0	6.5	6.5
Black locust	203,241	0.2	8.3	8.3
Black oak	162,593	0.3	10.3	9.0
Black tupelo	2,665,226	0.6	3.4	3.6
Black walnut	203,241	0.5	12.3	11.5
Black willow	40,648	0.1	9.5	9.5
Boxelder	569,075	1.1	10.3	8.0
Callery pear	1,277,461	0.4	3.6	4.2
Cherry	81,296	0.1	10.0	10.0
Chestnut oak	447,131	2.1	17.4	17.5
Chinese privet	3,141,364	0.2	1.6	1.5
Chinkapin oak	121,945	0.5	15.8	17.5
Eastern cottonwood	162,593	1.1	20.5	18.0
Eastern redbud	1,591,006	0.1	1.8	0.0
Eastern redcedar	3,611,777	1.7	4.7	3.7
Eastern white pine	121,945	0.3	12.8	12.5
Elm	81,296	0.6	22.0	21.0
Flowering dogwood	4,459,475	0.9	3.0	2.7
Green ash	638,731	0.2	2.4	0.0
Hackberry	243,889	0.2	6.5	6.5
Loblolly pine	325,186	1.1	14.0	11.0
Mockernut hickory	1,277,461	0.5	3.8	3.2
Transportation (continued)				
Mulberry	516,786	0.0	1.5	1.5
Northern red oak	40,648	0.1	10.5	10.5
Norway maple	40,648	0.0	6.5	6.5
Pecan	81,296	0.4	17.0	14.0
Pignut hickory	598,082	0.4	5.0	3.6
Post oak	81,296	0.1	10.5	10.0
Red maple	720,027	0.3	3.3	1.7
Red mulberry	40,648	0.0	5.5	5.5
Sassafras	516,786	0.0	1.5	1.5
Scarlet oak	40,648	0.0	8.5	8.5
Serviceberry	40,648	0.0	6.5	6.5
Shagbark hickory	365,834	0.3	7.6	7.5
Shortleaf pine	121,945	0.3	12.8	13.5
Silver maple	691,020	1.2	10.0	8.5
Slippery elm	40,648	0.0	6.5	6.5
Sourwood	121,945	0.1	6.8	6.5
Southern crabapple	81,296	0.0	6.0	6.0
Southern magnolia	121,945	0.2	9.5	7.5
Southern red oak	121,945	0.4	14.5	11.5
Sugar maple	1,834,896	0.5	4.0	3.8
Sugarberry	760,675	0.6	4.3	0.0
Sweetbay	720,027	0.2	4.1	3.7
Sweetgum	638,731	0.5	5.4	3.6
Sycamore	81,296	0.2	11.5	7.0
Tree-of-heaven	40,648	0.1	9.5	9.5
Virginia pine	8,088,618	2.7	2.9	1.7
Weeping willow	40,648	0.3	21.5	21.5
White ash	81,296	0.1	6.5	6.5
White mulberry	40,648	0.0	7.5	7.5
White oak	609,724	1.7	12.4	12.4
Willow oak	81,296	0.3	13.5	6.0
Winged elm	1,033,572	0.1	2.5	2.0
Yellow buckeye	2,148,440	0.4	2.5	2.1
Yellow-poplar	487,779	0.9	10.3	7.0

D.b.h. = Diameter at breast height.

Appendix E—Percent of Species Population Identified with Various Damage Type or Maintenance or Site Issue

Table E.1—Percent of species population identified with various damage type or maintenance or site issue, Tennessee, 2005–09

Species	Sample	Borers/ bark beetles	Canker/ decay	Chlorotic/ necrotic foliage	Dead top	Defoliation	Dead/ dying crown	Root/ stem girdling	Trunk/ bark inclusion	Vines in crown	Wound/ crack	Improper planting	Excess mulch	Overhead wires	Sidewalk- root conflict	Topping/ pruning
	n	----------						----	*percent*	---					----------	
American basswood	1	0.0	0.0	0.0	0.0	0.0	0.0	0.0	0.0	0.0	0.0	0.0	0.0	0.0	0.0	0.0
American beech	27	0.0	0.4	0.0	5.1	5.1	0.0	0.0	25.5	20.4	0.0	0.0	0.0	0.0	0.0	0.0
American elm	50	0.0	0.7	16.1	0.7	9.3	1.5	0.0	1.4	12.0	0.0	0.0	0.0	0.0	0.6	0.0
American holly	2	0.0	0.0	0.0	0.0	0.0	0.0	0.0	50.0	0.0	0.0	0.0	0.0	0.0	0.0	0.0
Amur honeysuckle	31	0.0	0.0	0.0	0.0	0.0	0.0	0.0	0.0	3.1	0.0	0.0	0.0	0.0	0.0	0.0
Baldcypress	10	0.0	0.0	0.0	0.0	0.0	0.0	0.0	0.0	0.0	0.0	0.0	0.0	0.0	0.0	0.0
Bitternut hickory	13	0.0	0.0	0.0	0.0	0.0	0.0	0.0	0.0	5.2	0.0	0.0	0.0	0.0	0.0	0.0
Black birch	1	0.0	0.0	0.0	0.0	0.0	0.0	0.0	0.0	0.0	0.0	0.0	0.0	0.0	0.0	0.0
Black cherry	83	0.0	3.5	1.8	6.5	11.3	6.6	0.0	2.1	24.7	0.0	0.0	0.0	0.0	0.4	0.5
Black locust	74	0.0	2.0	0.5	0.9	0.4	1.9	0.0	7.3	13.5	1.3	0.0	0.0	0.4	0.0	0.0
Black oak	33	0.0	0.0	0.0	3.5	0.0	10.0	0.0	6.0	0.0	3.0	0.0	0.0	0.0	0.0	0.0
Black tupelo	41	0.0	0.4	0.0	0.0	0.0	0.0	0.0	10.5	0.9	0.4	0.0	0.0	0.0	0.0	0.0
Black walnut	36	0.0	2.5	0.0	0.0	2.8	14.0	0.0	5.7	16.2	5.8	0.0	0.0	3.3	0.0	3.3
Black willow	8	0.0	0.0	0.0	0.0	0.0	12.3	0.0	24.6	0.0	0.0	0.0	0.0	0.0	0.0	0.0
Blackjack oak	4	0.0	0.0	0.0	0.0	0.0	0.0	0.0	0.0	0.0	0.0	0.0	0.0	0.0	0.0	0.0
Blue ash	3	0.0	0.0	0.0	0.0	0.0	0.0	0.0	66.7	0.0	33.3	0.0	0.0	0.0	0.0	0.0
Boxelder	52	0.0	7.7	0.0	2.1	0.9	3.0	0.0	5.0	5.0	0.0	0.0	0.0	2.1	0.0	1.0
Bur oak	1	0.0	0.0	0.0	0.0	0.0	0.0	0.0	0.0	0.0	0.0	0.0	0.0	0.0	0.0	0.0
Butternut	3	0.0	0.0	0.0	0.0	0.0	0.0	0.0	0.0	0.0	0.0	0.0	0.0	0.0	0.0	0.0
Callery pear	15	0.0	0.0	0.0	0.0	1.3	0.0	23.3	60.8	0.0	23.3	0.0	0.0	1.3	0.0	0.0
Carolina hemlock	1	0.0	0.0	0.0	0.0	0.0	0.0	0.0	0.0	0.0	0.0	0.0	0.0	0.0	0.0	0.0
Cherry	3	32.9	0.0	0.0	0.0	0.0	0.0	0.0	32.9	0.0	100.0	0.0	0.0	33.6	0.0	0.0
Cherrybark oak	12	0.7	0.7	0.0	0.0	0.0	0.0	0.0	8.4	25.2	0.7	0.0	0.0	0.0	0.0	2.7
Chestnut oak	86	0.7	0.0	0.0	0.0	0.7	0.8	0.7	4.8	0.0	0.0	0.0	0.0	0.0	0.0	0.0
Chinese chestnut	3	0.0	0.0	0.0	0.0	0.0	32.1	0.0	0.0	0.0	0.0	0.0	0.0	0.0	0.0	0.0
Chinese privet	73	0.0	0.0	0.0	0.0	0.0	0.0	0.0	4.7	11.7	1.5	2.7	0.0	0.0	0.0	2.7
Chinkapin oak	18	0.0	0.0	0.0	0.0	3.3	0.0	0.0	0.0	0.0	0.0	0.0	0.0	0.0	0.0	0.0
Cockspur hawthorn	6	0.0	0.0	0.0	0.0	0.0	0.0	0.0	0.0	0.0	2.4	0.0	0.0	0.0	0.0	0.0
Common cherry laurel	5	0.0	0.0	0.0	0.0	0.0	0.0	0.0	0.0	0.0	3.5	0.0	0.0	0.0	0.0	3.5
Common persimmon	13	0.0	0.0	0.0	1.6	0.0	1.6	0.0	1.4	3.0	1.4	0.0	0.0	0.0	0.0	0.0
Common plum	2	0.0	0.0	0.0	0.0	0.0	0.0	0.0	7.3	0.0	0.0	0.0	0.0	0.0	0.0	0.0
Crabapple	3	0.0	0.0	0.0	0.0	0.0	0.0	0.0	100.0	0.0	0.0	0.0	0.0	0.0	0.0	0.0
Dahoon	2	0.0	0.0	0.0	0.0	0.0	0.0	0.0	50.0	0.0	0.0	0.0	0.0	0.0	0.0	0.0

continued

Table E.1—Percent of species population identified with various damage type or maintenance or site issue, Tennessee, 2005–09 (continued)

		Damage type										Maintenance or site issue				
Species	Sample	Borers/bark beetles	Canker/decay	Chlorotic/necrotic foliage	Dead top	Defoliation	Dead/dying crown	Root/stem girdling	Trunk/bark inclusion	Vines in crown	Wound/crack	Improper planting	Excess mulch	Overhead wires	Sidewalk-root conflict	Topping/pruning
	n								— percent —							
Eastern cottonwood	7	0.0	0.0	0.0	0.0	0.0	0.0	0.0	0.0	30.8	14.7	0.0	0.0	0.0	0.0	0.0
Eastern hemlock	1	0.0	0.0	0.0	0.0	0.0	0.0	0.0	0.0	0.0	0.0	0.0	0.0	0.0	0.0	0.0
Eastern hophornbeam	7	0.0	0.0	0.0	0.0	0.0	0.0	0.0	0.0	24.2	0.0	0.0	0.0	0.0	0.0	0.0
Eastern redbud	27	0.0	1.9	0.0	14.1	8.8	11.8	0.0	18.1	1.6	1.7	0.0	0.0	1.6	0.0	0.0
Eastern redcedar	150	0.0	0.2	0.0	0.0	0.0	6.3	0.0	1.7	20.6	1.9	0.0	0.0	0.2	0.0	0.2
Eastern white pine	14	0.0	0.0	0.0	0.0	0.0	0.0	0.0	31.7	0.0	0.0	0.0	0.0	7.2	0.0	14.4
Elm	2	0.0	50.0	0.0	0.0	0.0	0.0	0.0	0.0	0.0	0.0	0.0	0.0	0.0	0.0	100.0
Flowering dogwood	51	0.0	8.4	3.7	0.4	0.0	0.4	0.0	27.8	0.3	0.9	0.0	0.0	4.6	0.0	1.1
Great leadtree	1	0.0	0.0	0.0	0.0	0.0	0.0	0.0	0.0	0.0	0.0	0.0	0.0	0.0	0.0	0.0
Green ash	38	0.0	1.1	0.0	0.0	14.4	0.0	0.0	0.0	2.3	0.0	0.0	0.0	0.0	0.0	0.0
Hackberry	145	3.0	6.7	0.0	0.5	0.0	7.1	0.2	10.8	14.8	1.9	0.0	0.0	0.5	0.3	1.0
Hawthorn	5	0.0	0.0	0.0	0.0	0.0	0.0	0.0	52.6	0.0	0.0	0.0	0.0	0.0	0.0	0.0
Honeylocust	4	0.0	0.0	0.0	0.0	0.0	0.0	0.0	0.0	0.0	0.0	0.0	0.0	0.0	0.0	0.0
Japanese privet	3	0.0	0.0	0.0	0.0	0.0	0.0	0.0	0.0	0.0	0.0	0.0	0.0	0.0	0.0	0.0
Loblolly pine	70	1.6	0.0	0.0	0.0	0.0	10.7	0.0	2.4	0.9	1.7	1.4	0.0	0.9	0.0	2.7
Longleaf pine	1	0.0	0.0	0.0	0.0	0.0	0.0	0.0	0.0	0.0	0.0	0.0	0.0	0.0	0.0	0.0
Mimosa	11	0.0	27.6	0.0	0.0	0.0	23.9	0.0	0.0	3.8	23.9	0.0	0.0	0.0	0.0	0.0
Mockernut hickory	31	0.0	1.8	0.0	0.0	12.0	0.8	0.0	0.0	1.1	0.9	0.0	0.0	0.0	0.0	0.0
Mulberry	1	0.0	0.0	0.0	0.0	0.0	0.0	0.0	0.0	0.0	0.0	0.0	0.0	0.0	0.0	0.0
Northern pin oak	3	0.0	0.0	0.0	0.0	66.7	0.0	0.0	0.0	0.0	0.0	0.0	0.0	0.0	0.0	0.0
Northern red oak	15	0.0	0.0	0.0	0.0	0.0	0.0	0.0	13.0	0.0	0.0	0.0	0.0	0.0	0.0	0.0
Northern white cedar	1	0.0	0.0	0.0	0.0	0.0	0.0	0.0	0.0	0.0	0.0	0.0	0.0	0.0	0.0	0.0
Norway maple	2	0.0	43.5	0.0	0.0	0.0	0.0	0.0	0.0	0.0	0.0	0.0	43.5	43.5	0.0	0.0
Osage orange	26	0.0	4.6	0.0	2.4	0.0	4.6	4.9	9.7	12.1	17.0	0.0	0.0	0.0	0.0	0.0
Other species	10	0.0	0.0	0.0	0.0	0.0	0.0	0.0	38.9	0.0	0.0	0.0	0.0	0.0	0.0	0.0
Pecan	12	0.0	10.5	0.0	0.0	9.5	8.2	0.0	26.4	8.2	0.0	0.0	0.0	14.7	0.0	7.3
Pignut hickory	38	0.0	0.7	0.0	0.0	0.0	0.7	0.0	3.0	0.0	0.7	0.0	0.0	0.0	0.0	0.0
Pin cherry	2	0.0	0.0	0.0	0.0	50.0	0.0	0.0	0.0	0.0	0.0	0.0	0.0	0.0	0.0	0.0
Pin oak	5	0.0	0.0	0.0	0.0	0.0	0.0	0.0	20.0	0.0	0.0	0.0	0.0	0.0	0.0	0.0
Post oak	18	0.0	5.5	5.0	0.0	0.0	16.6	0.0	5.5	0.0	10.5	0.0	0.0	0.0	0.0	5.0
Red maple	68	0.0	5.8	0.0	5.1	0.0	5.5	0.3	13.1	0.0	0.7	0.0	0.7	0.7	0.0	0.0
Red mulberry	9	4.8	4.8	0.0	0.0	0.0	5.2	0.0	0.0	5.2	0.0	0.0	0.0	0.0	0.0	0.0
Sassafras	40	0.0	1.2	0.0	2.7	0.0	9.1	0.0	0.0	6.8	2.7	0.0	0.0	0.0	0.0	0.0

continued

Table E.1—Percent of species population identified with various damage type or maintenance or site issue, Tennessee, 2005–09 (continued)

Species	Sample n	Damage type										Maintenance or site issue				
		Borers/bark beetles	Canker/decay	Chlorotic/necrotic foliage	Dead top	Defoliation	Dead/dying crown	Root/stem girdling	Trunk/bark inclusion	Vines in crown	Wound/crack	Improper planting	Excess mulch	Overhead wires	Sidewalk-root conflict	Topping/pruning
		- percent -														
Scarlet oak	9	0.0	0.0	0.0	0.0	0.0	0.0	0.0	0.0	0.0	10.4	0.0	0.0	22.5	0.0	12.1
Serviceberry	2	0.0	0.0	0.0	0.0	0.0	0.0	0.0	0.0	0.0	0.0	0.0	0.0	0.0	0.0	0.0
Shagbark hickory	27	0.0	8.7	0.0	28.3	0.0	0.0	0.0	2.2	0.0	0.0	0.0	0.0	0.0	0.0	0.0
Shortleaf pine	23	0.0	0.0	0.0	2.1	0.0	0.0	0.0	4.3	0.0	0.0	0.0	0.0	0.0	0.0	0.0
Shumard oak	3	0.0	0.0	0.0	0.0	0.0	0.0	0.0	0.0	0.0	0.0	0.0	0.0	0.0	0.0	0.0
Siberian elm	6	0.0	30.9	13.6	0.0	0.0	0.0	0.0	0.0	34.6	17.3	0.0	0.0	13.6	0.0	0.0
Silver maple	70	5.5	6.4	0.0	2.7	0.0	5.4	0.0	14.7	4.6	5.3	0.0	0.0	5.4	0.0	0.0
Slippery elm	25	0.0	0.0	0.8	0.0	0.8	1.5	0.0	0.0	4.7	0.0	0.0	0.0	0.0	0.0	0.0
Smoke tree	3	0.0	0.0	0.0	0.0	0.0	0.0	0.0	33.3	0.0	0.0	0.0	0.0	0.0	0.0	0.0
Sourwood	41	0.0	13.1	0.7	1.5	1.6	11.7	0.0	0.0	1.5	10.1	1.5	0.0	1.5	1.5	0.0
Southern catalpa	2	0.0	0.0	0.0	0.0	0.0	0.0	0.0	0.0	91.9	8.1	0.0	0.0	0.0	0.0	0.0
Southern crabapple	2	0.0	50.0	0.0	0.0	0.0	0.0	0.0	100.0	0.0	0.0	0.0	0.0	0.0	0.0	0.0
Southern magnolia	5	0.0	44.0	0.0	0.0	0.0	0.0	0.0	44.0	0.0	0.0	0.0	0.0	0.0	0.0	0.0
Southern red oak	31	0.0	2.1	0.0	0.0	0.0	0.0	0.0	1.8	3.5	1.8	0.0	0.0	4.5	0.0	0.0
Sugar maple	72	0.0	1.7	0.0	0.0	0.0	0.4	0.0	2.0	5.7	0.4	0.0	0.0	0.0	0.0	0.0
Sugarberry	32	0.0	2.2	0.0	1.1	2.4	1.1	1.1	2.2	1.3	4.9	0.0	0.0	0.0	0.0	3.3
Swamp chestnut oak	1	0.0	0.0	0.0	0.0	0.0	0.0	0.0	0.0	0.0	0.0	0.0	0.0	0.0	0.0	0.0
Sweet cherry	3	0.0	0.0	0.0	0.0	0.0	0.0	0.0	11.0	0.0	0.0	0.0	0.0	0.0	0.0	0.0
Sweetbay	6	0.0	0.0	0.0	0.0	0.0	0.0	0.0	100.0	0.0	0.0	0.0	0.0	0.0	0.0	0.0
Sweetgum	73	0.0	6.3	0.0	10.7	0.0	17.5	0.4	0.0	8.8	5.0	0.0	0.0	0.4	0.0	0.0
Sycamore	14	0.0	4.1	3.2	0.0	0.0	8.3	0.0	60.8	0.0	4.1	0.0	0.0	0.0	0.0	3.8
Tree-of-heaven	10	0.0	0.0	0.0	0.0	0.0	0.0	0.0	0.0	0.0	3.7	0.0	0.0	0.0	0.0	0.0
Virginia pine	132	0.0	6.6	0.0	0.0	0.0	0.2	0.0	12.3	5.5	0.2	0.0	0.0	0.6	0.2	0.2
Water oak	13	0.0	0.0	0.0	6.7	0.0	8.6	12.1	29.4	15.4	6.7	0.0	0.0	12.1	0.0	0.0
Weeping willow	1	0.0	0.0	0.0	0.0	0.0	0.0	0.0	0.0	0.0	100.0	0.0	0.0	0.0	0.0	0.0
White ash	37	0.0	0.0	0.0	1.5	0.0	0.0	3.1	0.0	6.3	0.0	0.0	0.0	0.0	1.5	0.0
White mulberry	3	0.0	0.0	0.0	0.0	0.0	0.0	0.0	0.0	0.0	0.0	0.0	0.0	0.0	0.0	0.0
White oak	58	0.0	1.2	0.0	1.2	0.0	1.4	0.0	4.0	2.4	0.0	0.0	0.0	0.0	0.0	0.0
Willow oak	5	0.0	20.1	0.0	0.0	9.4	0.0	0.0	0.0	18.9	0.0	0.0	0.0	17.0	0.0	17.0
Winged elm	70	0.0	0.4	0.0	0.0	0.0	5.1	0.0	0.0	21.4	2.2	0.0	0.0	0.0	0.0	0.0
Yellow buckeye	6	0.0	1.9	0.0	0.0	0.0	0.0	0.0	24.1	0.0	0.0	0.0	0.0	0.0	0.0	0.0
Yellow-poplar	100	0.0	4.2	0.0	0.0	0.6	0.6	0.0	2.8	1.1	2.8	0.0	0.0	0.0	0.0	0.0
Yellowwood	1	0.0	0.0	0.0	0.0	0.0	0.0	0.0	100.0	0.0	100.0	0.0	0.0	0.0	0.0	0.0
All trees		0.3	2.9	0.6	1.6	1.6	3.2	0.3	8.7	7.9	2.1	0.3	0.0	0.7	0.1	0.7

Table F.1—Percent of population of trees with damage type or maintenance or site issue occupied by individual species (i.e., sum of column adds to 100 percent), Tennessee, 2005–09

Species	Damage type											Maintenance or site issue			
	Borers/bark beetles	Canker/decay	Chlorotic/necrotic foliage	Dead top	Defoliation	Dead/dying crown	Root/stem girdling	Trunk/bark inclusion	Vines in crown	Wound/crack	Improper planting	Excess mulch	Overhead wires	Sidewalk-root conflict	Topping/pruning
	percent														
American basswood	0.0	0.0	0.0	0.0	0.0	0.0	0.0	0.0	0.0	0.0	0.0	0.0	0.0	0.0	0.0
American beech	5.8	0.0	0.4	0.0	9.9	9.5	0.0	0.0	9.0	7.9	0.0	0.0	0.0	0.0	0.0
American elm	2.9	0.0	0.4	49.0	0.8	10.3	0.0	0.0	0.3	2.8	0.8	0.0	0.0	0.0	13.1
American holly	0.0	0.0	0.0	0.0	0.0	0.0	0.0	0.0	0.1	0.0	0.0	0.0	0.0	0.0	0.0
Amur honeysuckle	0.6	0.0	0.0	0.0	0.0	0.0	0.0	0.0	0.0	1.8	0.0	0.0	0.0	0.0	0.0
Baldcypress	0.0	0.0	0.0	0.0	0.0	0.0	0.0	0.0	0.0	0.0	0.0	0.0	0.0	0.0	0.0
Bitternut hickory	0.1	0.0	0.0	0.0	0.0	0.0	0.0	0.0	0.0	0.2	0.0	0.0	0.0	0.0	0.0
Black birch	0.0	0.0	0.0	0.0	0.0	0.0	0.0	0.0	0.0	0.0	0.0	0.0	0.0	0.0	0.0
Black cherry	6.0	0.0	3.3	8.4	11.3	19.0	1.6	2.1	0.7	8.6	5.6	0.0	0.0	0.0	13.1
Black locust	2.8	0.0	1.9	2.2	1.6	0.7	0.0	0.0	2.3	4.8	1.7	0.0	0.0	0.0	0.0
Black oak	0.3	0.0	0.0	0.0	0.9	0.0	0.0	0.0	0.3	0.0	1.3	0.0	0.0	0.0	0.0
Black tupelo	1.5	0.0	0.4	0.0	0.0	0.0	0.0	0.0	3.7	0.3	0.0	0.0	0.0	0.0	0.0
Black walnut	0.6	0.0	0.4	0.0	0.0	0.7	2.0	2.1	0.3	0.9	1.9	0.0	0.0	0.0	0.0
Black willow	0.1	0.0	0.0	0.0	0.0	0.0	0.0	0.0	0.3	0.0	0.4	0.0	0.0	0.0	0.0
Blackjack oak	0.0	0.0	0.0	0.0	0.0	0.0	0.0	0.0	0.0	0.0	0.0	0.0	0.0	0.0	0.0
Blue ash	0.2	0.0	0.0	0.0	0.0	0.0	0.0	0.0	0.3	0.0	0.0	0.0	0.0	0.0	0.0
Boxelder	1.0	0.0	3.7	0.0	1.8	0.8	4.1	2.1	0.8	0.9	1.3	0.0	0.0	0.0	0.0
Bur oak	0.0	0.0	0.0	0.0	0.0	0.0	0.0	0.0	0.0	0.0	0.0	0.0	0.0	0.0	0.0
Butternut	0.0	0.0	0.0	0.0	0.0	0.0	0.0	0.0	0.0	0.0	0.0	0.0	0.0	0.0	0.0
Callery pear	2.1	0.0	0.0	0.0	0.0	0.7	1.6	0.0	6.0	0.0	0.0	0.0	0.0	61.1	0.0
Carolina hemlock	0.0	0.0	0.0	0.0	0.0	0.0	0.0	0.0	0.0	0.0	0.0	0.0	0.0	0.0	0.0
Cherry	0.2	0.0	0.5	0.0	0.0	0.0	2.0	0.0	0.2	0.0	0.0	0.0	0.0	0.0	0.0
Cherrybark oak	0.2	0.0	0.0	0.0	0.0	0.0	0.0	0.0	0.1	0.5	0.0	0.0	0.0	0.0	0.0
Chestnut oak	0.5	4.5	0.4	0.0	0.0	0.7	0.0	0.0	1.0	0.0	0.4	0.0	0.0	3.7	0.0
Chinese chestnut	0.0	0.0	0.0	0.0	0.0	0.0	0.0	0.0	0.0	0.0	0.3	0.0	0.0	0.0	0.0
Chinese privet	7.4	0.0	0.0	0.0	0.0	0.0	0.0	42.0	5.7	15.4	0.0	85.7	0.0	0.0	0.0
Chinkapin oak	0.1	0.0	0.0	0.0	0.0	0.7	0.0	0.0	0.0	0.0	0.0	0.0	0.0	0.0	0.0
Cockspur hawthorn	0.1	0.0	0.0	0.0	0.0	0.0	0.0	0.0	0.0	0.0	0.0	0.0	0.0	0.0	0.0
Common cherry laurel	0.0	0.0	0.0	0.0	0.0	0.0	0.0	1.7	0.0	0.0	0.0	0.0	0.0	0.0	0.0
Common persimmon	0.2	0.0	0.0	0.0	0.8	0.0	0.0	0.0	0.1	0.3	0.4	0.0	0.0	0.0	0.0
Common plum	0.1	0.0	0.0	0.0	0.0	0.0	0.0	0.0	0.1	0.0	0.0	0.0	0.0	0.0	0.0
Crabapple	0.1	0.0	0.0	0.0	0.0	0.0	0.0	0.0	0.4	0.0	0.0	0.0	0.0	0.0	0.0
Dahoon	0.0	0.0	0.0	0.0	0.0	0.0	0.0	0.0	0.1	0.0	0.0	0.0	0.0	0.0	0.0

continued

Table F.1—Percent of population of trees with damage type or maintenance or site issue occupied by individual species (i.e., sum of column adds to 100 percent), Tennessee, 2005–09 (continued)

Species	Damage type											Maintenance or site issue			
	Borers/ bark beetles	Canker/ decay	Chlorotic/ necrotic foliage	Dead top	Defoliation	Dead/ dying crown	Root/ stem girdling	Trunk/ bark inclusion	Vines in crown	Wound/ crack	Improper planting	Excess mulch	Overhead wires	Sidewalk- root conflict	Topping/ pruning
	percent														
Eastern cottonwood	0.2	0.0	0.0	0.0	0.0	0.0	0.0	0.0	0.0	0.4	0.0	0.0	0.0	0.0	0.0
Eastern hemlock	0.0	0.0	0.0	0.0	0.0	0.0	0.0	0.0	0.0	0.0	0.0	0.0	0.0	0.0	0.0
Eastern hophornbeam	0.6	0.0	0.0	0.0	0.0	0.0	0.0	0.0	0.0	2.0	0.0	0.0	0.0	0.0	0.0
Eastern redbud	3.0	0.0	1.4	0.0	18.5	11.1	4.7	0.0	4.3	0.4	7.6	0.0	0.0	0.0	0.0
Eastern redcedar	6.8	0.0	0.5	0.0	0.0	0.0	2.0	2.1	1.2	15.5	11.7	0.0	0.0	0.0	0.0
Eastern white pine	0.4	0.0	0.0	0.0	0.0	0.0	2.0	4.3	0.7	0.0	0.0	0.0	0.0	0.0	0.0
Elm	0.1	0.0	0.5	0.0	0.0	0.0	0.0	4.3	0.0	0.0	0.0	0.0	0.0	0.0	0.0
Flowering dogwood	8.1	0.0	14.3	30.5	1.4	0.0	32.2	8.3	15.7	0.2	0.7	0.0	0.0	0.0	0.0
Great leadtree	0.0	0.0	0.0	0.0	0.0	9.5	0.0	0.0	0.0	0.0	0.0	0.0	0.0	0.0	0.0
Green ash	0.8	0.0	0.4	0.0	0.0	9.5	0.0	0.0	0.0	0.3	0.0	0.0	0.0	0.0	18.7
Hackberry	7.5	57.1	12.1	0.0	1.5	0.0	3.8	8.1	6.5	9.8	11.5	0.0	0.0	3.7	18.7
Hawthorn	1.5	0.0	0.0	0.0	0.0	0.0	0.0	0.0	4.3	0.0	0.0	0.0	0.0	0.0	0.0
Honeylocust	0.0	0.0	0.0	0.0	0.0	0.0	0.0	0.0	0.0	0.0	0.0	0.0	0.0	0.0	0.0
Japanese privet	0.0	0.0	0.0	0.0	0.0	0.0	0.0	0.0	0.0	0.0	0.0	0.0	0.0	0.0	0.0
Loblolly pine	1.1	9.3	0.0	0.0	0.0	0.0	2.0	6.4	0.4	0.2	5.3	6.8	0.0	0.0	0.0
Longleaf pine	0.0	0.0	0.0	0.0	0.0	0.0	0.0	0.0	0.0	0.0	0.0	0.0	0.0	0.0	0.0
Mimosa	0.8	0.0	5.6	0.0	0.0	0.0	0.0	0.0	0.0	0.3	4.3	0.0	0.0	0.0	0.0
Mockernut hickory	0.9	0.0	0.8	0.0	0.0	9.5	0.0	0.0	0.0	0.2	0.3	0.0	0.0	0.0	0.0
Mulberry	0.0	0.0	0.0	0.0	0.0	0.0	0.0	0.0	0.0	0.0	0.0	0.0	0.0	0.0	0.0
Northern pin oak	0.1	0.0	0.0	0.0	0.0	1.3	0.0	0.0	0.0	0.0	0.0	0.0	0.0	0.0	0.0
Northern red oak	0.1	0.0	0.0	0.0	0.0	0.0	0.0	0.0	0.3	0.0	0.0	0.0	0.0	0.0	0.0
Northern white cedar	0.0	0.0	0.0	0.0	0.0	0.0	0.0	0.0	0.0	0.0	0.0	0.0	0.0	0.0	0.0
Norway maple	0.0	0.0	0.4	0.0	0.0	0.0	1.6	0.0	0.0	0.0	0.0	0.0	33.3	0.0	0.0
Osage orange	0.6	0.0	0.8	0.0	0.8	0.0	0.0	0.0	0.6	0.8	0.7	0.0	0.0	7.5	0.0
Other species	0.4	0.0	0.0	0.0	0.0	0.0	0.0	0.0	1.1	0.0	0.0	0.0	0.0	0.0	0.0
Pecan	0.3	0.0	0.5	0.0	0.0	0.9	3.1	1.7	0.5	0.2	0.4	0.0	0.0	0.0	0.0
Pignut hickory	0.4	0.0	0.4	0.0	0.0	0.0	0.0	0.0	0.6	0.0	0.4	0.0	0.0	0.0	0.0
Pin cherry	0.1	0.0	0.0	0.0	0.0	0.7	0.0	0.0	0.1	0.0	0.0	0.0	0.0	0.0	0.0
Pin oak	0.0	0.0	0.0	0.0	0.0	0.0	0.0	0.0	0.1	0.0	0.0	0.0	0.0	0.0	0.0
Post oak	0.3	0.0	0.4	1.9	0.0	0.0	0.0	1.7	0.1	0.0	1.1	0.0	0.0	0.0	0.0
Red maple	3.3	0.0	6.6	0.0	10.6	0.0	3.1	0.0	5.0	0.0	5.6	0.0	66.7	3.4	0.0
Red mulberry	0.1	4.5	0.4	0.0	0.0	0.0	0.0	0.0	0.0	0.2	0.4	0.0	0.0	0.0	0.0
Sassafras	0.6	0.0	0.4	0.0	1.6	0.0	0.0	0.0	0.0	0.8	2.6	0.0	0.0	0.0	0.0

continued

Table F.1—Percent of population of trees with damage type or maintenance or site issue occupied by individual species (i.e., sum of column adds to 100 percent), Tennessee, 2005–09 (continued)

Species	Damage type										Maintenance or site issue				
	Borers/ bark beetles	Canker/ decay	Chlorotic/ necrotic foliage	Dead top	Defoliation	Dead/ dying crown	Root/ stem girdling	Trunk/ bark inclusion	Vines in crown	Wound/ crack	Improper planting	Excess mulch	Overhead wires	Sidewalk- root conflict	Topping/ pruning
	percent														
Scarlet oak	0.1	0.0	0.0	0.0	0.0	0.0	3.8	2.1	0.0	0.0	0.0	0.0	0.0	0.0	0.0
Serviceberry	0.0	0.0	0.0	0.0	0.0	0.0	0.0	0.0	0.0	0.0	0.0	0.0	0.0	0.0	0.0
Shagbark hickory	1.0	0.0	1.9	0.0	11.4	0.0	0.0	0.0	0.2	0.0	0.0	0.0	0.0	0.0	0.0
Shortleaf pine	0.2	0.0	0.0	0.0	0.8	0.0	0.0	0.0	0.3	0.0	0.0	0.0	0.0	0.0	0.0
Shumard oak	0.0	0.0	0.0	0.0	0.0	0.0	0.0	0.0	0.0	0.0	0.0	0.0	0.0	0.0	0.0
Siberian elm	0.2	0.0	0.9	1.9	0.0	0.0	1.6	0.0	0.0	0.4	0.0	0.0	0.0	0.0	0.0
Silver maple	1.6	24.7	2.7	0.0	2.1	0.0	9.4	0.0	2.1	0.7	2.0	0.0	0.0	0.0	0.0
Slippery elm	0.3	0.0	0.0	2.1	0.0	0.7	0.0	0.0	0.0	0.9	0.7	0.0	0.0	0.0	0.0
Smoke tree	0.6	0.0	0.0	0.0	0.0	0.0	0.0	0.0	1.8	0.0	0.0	0.0	0.0	0.0	0.0
Sourwood	2.3	0.0	7.5	2.1	1.6	1.6	3.5	0.0	0.0	0.3	6.0	7.5	0.0	0.0	29.1
Southern catalpa	0.6	0.0	0.0	0.0	0.0	0.0	0.0	0.0	0.0	1.8	0.0	0.0	0.0	0.0	0.0
Southern crabapple	0.1	0.0	0.5	0.0	0.0	0.0	0.0	0.0	0.3	0.0	0.0	0.0	0.0	0.0	0.0
Southern magnolia	0.2	0.0	1.0	0.0	0.0	0.0	0.0	0.0	0.3	0.0	0.0	0.0	0.0	0.0	0.0
Southern red oak	0.2	0.0	0.5	0.0	0.0	0.0	4.5	0.0	0.1	0.3	0.0	0.0	0.0	0.0	0.0
Sugar maple	1.1	0.0	1.7	0.0	0.0	0.0	0.0	0.0	0.7	2.1	0.3	0.0	0.0	0.0	0.0
Sugarberry	0.4	0.0	0.8	0.0	0.7	1.5	0.0	5.0	0.3	0.2	0.3	0.0	0.0	3.4	0.0
Swamp chestnut oak	0.0	0.0	0.0	0.0	0.0	0.0	0.0	0.0	0.0	0.0	0.0	0.0	0.0	0.0	0.0
Sweet cherry	0.1	0.0	0.0	0.0	0.0	0.0	0.0	0.0	0.3	0.0	0.0	0.0	0.0	0.0	0.0
Sweetbay	1.0	0.0	0.0	0.0	0.0	0.0	0.0	0.0	2.9	0.0	0.0	0.0	0.0	0.0	0.0
Sweetgum	4.4	0.0	6.3	0.0	19.8	0.0	1.6	0.0	0.0	3.2	15.8	0.0	0.0	3.7	0.0
Sycamore	1.2	0.0	0.5	2.1	0.0	0.0	0.0	2.1	2.7	0.0	1.0	0.0	0.0	0.0	0.0
Tree-of-heaven	0.1	0.0	0.0	0.0	0.0	0.0	0.0	0.0	0.0	0.0	0.0	0.0	0.0	0.0	0.0
Virginia pine	5.4	0.0	13.7	0.0	0.0	0.0	5.2	2.1	8.5	4.2	0.4	0.0	0.0	0.0	13.1
Water oak	0.4	0.0	0.0	0.0	0.8	0.0	3.1	0.0	0.6	0.4	0.5	0.0	0.0	6.7	0.0
Weeping willow	0.1	0.0	0.0	0.0	0.0	0.0	0.0	0.0	0.0	0.0	0.0	0.0	0.0	0.0	0.0
White ash	0.3	0.0	0.0	0.0	0.7	0.0	0.0	0.0	0.0	0.6	0.0	0.0	0.0	6.7	13.1
White mulberry	0.0	0.0	0.0	0.0	0.0	0.0	0.0	0.0	0.0	0.0	0.0	0.0	0.0	0.0	0.0
White oak	0.4	0.0	0.4	0.0	0.8	0.0	0.0	0.0	0.5	0.3	0.4	0.0	0.0	0.0	0.0
Willow oak	0.1	0.0	0.5	0.0	0.0	0.0	1.6	1.7	0.0	0.2	0.0	0.0	0.0	0.0	0.0
Winged elm	3.9	0.0	0.4	0.0	0.0	19.0	0.0	0.0	0.0	8.9	5.2	0.0	0.0	0.0	0.0
Yellow buckeye	0.8	0.0	0.5	0.0	0.0	0.0	0.0	0.0	2.1	0.0	0.0	0.0	0.0	0.0	0.0
Yellow-poplar	1.1	0.0	3.2	0.0	0.0	0.7	0.0	0.0	0.7	0.3	0.4	0.0	0.0	0.0	0.0
Yellowwood	0.8	0.0	0.0	0.0	0.0	0.0	0.0	0.0	2.3	0.0	0.0	0.0	0.0	0.0	0.0